# THIS IS MORE
# THAN I CAN STAND

*A Biography of Charlie Hall*

# THIS IS MORE THAN I CAN STAND

## *A Biography of Charlie Hall*

John Ullah

BREWIN BOOKS

First published by
Brewin Books Ltd, 56 Alcester Road,
Studley, Warwickshire B80 7LG in 2012
www.brewinbooks.com

Reprinted June 2014

ISBN: 978-1-85858-483-6

A Cataloguing in Publication Record
for this title is available from the British Library.

Front cover images:
Top: Stan and Ollie point the finger of blame at Charlie in 'Tit For Tat'.
Bottom: New Street in the early twentieth century, taken from
*Streets of Brum, Part Four* by Carl Chinn, published by Brewin Books.

Typeset in New Baskerville
Printed in Great Britain by
4edge Ltd.

# TABLE OF CONTENTS

*This book is dedicated to Barrie Finney.*

# SHAKESPEARE AND SHORT FELLOW

William Shakespeare – you may have heard of him – was a bit of a compulsive writer. He simply couldn't put down his quill. Play after play after play, 37 of them to be precise. When I was at school, the English syllabus was such that we poor students had to study many of these in great detail. There were the tragedies, which were ultra depressing (who the heck was Coriolanus?), the histories which sent me to sleep (Henry the Tenth Part 22 etc.) and the comedies. Now I thought I would at least enjoy the "comedies". But to paraphrase Shakespeare himself, I found they were Much Ado About Bugger All. I didn't laugh at them.

This brings me on to the Short Fellow. When I was about 10 years old, I discovered Laurel and Hardy at Saturday Morning Pictures. Now that was proper comedy and that did make me laugh then – and still does today (in case you are wondering, today is Tuesday). I took far more interest in Laurel and Hardy than Shakespeare. I wanted to learn more about them; where did they come from, how did they get together and who was the funny Short Fellow in their films?

Time passed and inevitably I found out more and more about Laurel and Hardy and remembered less and less about Shakespeare. I bought myself John McCabe's pioneering book, Mr Laurel and Mr Hardy, occasionally saw a Laurel and Hardy feature film at the cinema and thoroughly enjoyed seeing their comedy classics revived on BBC2 television. I was now aware that the Short Fellow in their films was called Charlie Hall but I still knew next to nothing about him.

Discovering the Sons of the Desert in 1989 reassured me that I was not a complete idiot in being so passionate about Laurel and Hardy. There were not just a few, but thousands of other fans who loved their comedy. Being a complete idiot came later! The Sons of the Desert – what an organisation: fans, friends and fun galore. Right from the off, I found myself chatting easily and readily to other Sons. I learnt quite a lot more about Laurel and Hardy and their co-stars. I now knew that Charlie Hall came from Birmingham, Warwickshire. (Isn't that the same county as where Mr Shakespeare was born?). I also met a young man from that same city who had also recently become a Son of the Desert. His name was John Ullah.

Talk about enthusiasm. John Ullah's cup is overflowing with the stuff. The Laughing Gravy Tent fronted by John and his partner Mandy Finney, achieved the seemingly impossible task of hosting the International Laurel and Hardy Convention in Birmingham in 1998. Ever since, they have excelled in all that they have done; raising money for the L & H statue in Ulverston, hosting a UK Convention, supporting many other Sons of the Desert events and holding monthly meetings with a huge audience. And everything they do is done with a smile, laughter and for the right reasons.

At the 1998 International Convention, John and his team showed a promotional video about Laurel and Hardy and the Birmingham connections. Scholarly Sons (oh, there are some) will know that is where John McCabe first saw Laurel & Hardy perform on stage. McCabe was studying Shakespeare at the time at University. I hope he enjoyed it more than I ever did. So Birmingham is where the Sons of the Desert really do have their roots as McCabe later went on to form our unique appreciation society. In the same video I learnt more about Charlie Hall; he was born nearby, there is a fire station on the site of his former home, and a relative was still working there as a fireman. I loved all of this and I knew that John Ullah had done meticulous research. Greedily I wanted to know more. I hoped that John could continue his research and maybe, just one day, he could write a book about the Brummie co-star who appeared in nearly 50 films with Laurel and Hardy. There has been a couple of books, some articles and filmographies but John Ullah always seemed like the right (or should that be write) person to tell us more about the Short Fellow. As always, John has come up trumps with "Charlie Hall – This is More Than I Can Stand".

If Shakespeare were alive today (did you know he died a while back?) perhaps he could write a comedy play about Charlie Hall called "Hall's Well That Ends Swell". I'm sure that would make me laugh but I bet he would need John's book.

*Roger Robinson*

# SHAKESPEARE AND SHORT FELLOW

*"I know you were hoping for 'Midlander of the Year' title Will, but you only wrote a few plays – I was on the Silver Screen with Laurel and Hardy – NO CONTEST."*

Tony Bagley

# INTRODUCTION

We all have our own favourites when it comes to comedy. The people who have made me laugh over the years are Spike Milligan, Eric Sykes, Ken Dodd, Tony Hancock, and Woody Allen to name a few. I also enjoy comedies such as Dad's Army, Rising Damp, Father Ted, Phoenix Nights, The Royle Family, Cheers and Frasier.

I think cartoons like The Simpsons, Bugs Bunny, Daffy Duck, Elmer Fudd are simply brilliant.

But there is one group of people who I have always put above all others. They are the great silent clowns of yesteryear. Laurel & Hardy, Charlie Chaplin, Buster Keaton, The Keystone Cops, Harry Langdon, Harold Lloyd, Roscoe 'Fatty' Arbuckle, Snub Pollard etc, etc etc. And of these, Laurel & Hardy have always been my favourites, simply because they were (and still are) funnier than anyone else.

I'm proud to say that Birmingham has strong connections with my two comedy heroes. The obvious being their association with Charlie Hall.

This book tells the story of Charlie's upbringing in Birmingham, through to his last known profession as a prop maker for Warner Bros. The book also contains details of where he worked, his return to Birmingham in 1937 and interviews with people who met him. It will correct much of the information that has been written about Charlie in the past, and it will shed new light on the little man from the Ward End district of Birmingham.

One of the rewards for writing this book has been meeting Charlie's relatives. His nephew, Bryan Hall, and nieces Joyce Perry and Jean Cook, are undoubtedly three of the nicest people that I have ever met.

All three are very proud of Charlie, albeit in a quiet and modest way. They are now my good friends, and I hope they enjoy reading about the incredible life of their 'Uncle Charlie'.

## Chapter One

# HIS BIRMINGHAM ROOTS

The year is 1931. The film is Laughing Gravy. Stan Laurel and Oliver Hardy are about to leave a boarding house.

"C'mon," says Charlie Hall, a double-barrelled shotgun in hand.

"Get out of here, and make it snappy."

(There's knocking on the door)

Charlie opens it to find a policeman (Harry Bernard), fixing a note to the door.

"Wait a minute," says the policeman, "This house is under quarantine. No one can leave here for two months."

"Two months?" yells Charlie.

"Two months," replies the policeman.

Charlie then utters one of his most famous lines: "This is more than I can stand!"

He heaves a big sigh, and dramatically exits to the left of the screen, dragging the shotgun behind him.

We hear two shots ring out (the first one obviously missed!) and Stan, Ollie and the policeman take off their hats, bow their heads and walk slowly out of shot.

A very funny ending to a very funny film.

So, how did Charlie Hall, a working-class man from a working-class area of Birmingham, come to appear with these two masters of comedy?

We'll start our story on 2nd August 1896. It was on this date that a certain Thomas Hall (aged 24) married Maria Reynolds (aged 22) at St. Mary's Church, in the parish of Aston Brook, Birmingham. Thomas lists his profession as a 'Carter' (his father George was a labourer). Maria's profession is not listed but her father (Charles) was a 'Milk Seller'. Like a lot of people in Victorian England at that time, Thomas Hall couldn't read or write, and on his Marriage Certificate he has simply put an 'X', (next to this the Registrar has written 'His Mark').

*Thomas and Maria Hall's marriage certificate.*

Thomas and Maria would go on to have eight children Herbert, Charles, Florence, Thomas (known as Walter), Harry, Arthur, Alfred and Frank. It would appear Maria named the children after members of her own family, as she had three brothers, called Walter, Herbert and Charles and a sister called Florence. She named her daughter Florence Matilda Hall to be exact (Matilda being Maria's mother's name).

The children were born in Gwyther Cottages, on the Washwood Heath Road, in the District of Ward End, Birmingham. The name 'Warde End' was first recorded in 1460. It was part of Little Bromwich, in the parish of Aston Manor. The name is thought to have been derived from the Ward family during the 13th century, the 'End' signifying a few cottages near the entrance to a church or a manor-house.

In 1884 Fredrick Gwyther bought three cottages in a sale from George William Marshall. The sale read:

**LOT 9.**

# THREE COTTAGES & GARDENS,

TOGETHER WITH A PLOT OF CHOICE

## BUILDING LAND,

Adjoining Lot 7, having a frontage of 54 yards to the Main Road, and containing 0a. 2r. 11p., or thereabouts.

NOTE.—This Lot will be Sold subject to the Cottages being pulled down within three years.

*Cottages for sale.*

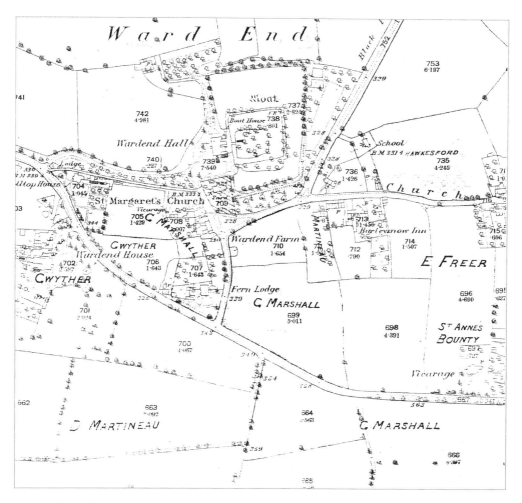

*Map of Ward End 1888.*

Lot 9
Three Cottages & Gardens
Together with a plot of choice Building Land
Adjoining Lot 7, having a frontage of 54 yards to the Main Road, and containing oa. 2r. 11p, or thereabouts.
Note – This lot will be sold subject to the Cottages being pulled down within three years.

We now know that this did not happen.

FD 235577

CERTIFIED COPY of an ENTRY
Pursuant to the Births and Deaths Registration Act 1953

**BIRTH**

REGISTRATION DISTRICT  Aston

1899. BIRTHS in the Sub-District of Erdington in the Counties of Warwick & Birmingham

| No. | When and Where Born. | Name, if any. | Sex. | Name and Surname of Father. | Name and Maiden Surname of Mother. | Rank or Profession of Father. | Signature, Description, and Residence of Informant. | When Registered. | Signature of Registrar. | Baptismal Name, if added after Registration of Birth. |
|---|---|---|---|---|---|---|---|---|---|---|
| 23 | Nineteenth August 1899 Washwood Heath Road Ward End u.B | Charles | Boy | Thomas Calvin Hall | Maria Hall formerly Reynolds | General Labourer | M Hall Mother Washwood Heath Road Ward End | Twenty ninth September 1899 | G.A.Machin Registrar | |

Certified to be a true copy of an entry in a register in my custody.

S. Muun Superintendent Registrar

15 . 8 . 2007 Date

CAUTION: THERE ARE OFFENCES RELATING TO FALSIFYING OR ALTERING A CERTIFICATE AND USING OR POSSESSING A FALSE CERTIFICATE. ©CROWN COPYRIGHT
WARNING: A CERTIFICATE IS NOT EVIDENCE OF IDENTITY.

*Charlie's birth certificate.*

It was in one of these cottages that Charles Hall (or Charlie as we now call him) was born. The date was 19th August 1899, and he was the second child of Thomas and Maria. He was baptised at St. Margaret's Church on 10th September 1899 by the Rev. Charles Heath. The Church Tower was visible from Charlie's home and all the children were baptised there with the exception of Frank. St Margaret's church still stands today.

In 1979 it was described as: "A small building by Rickman in the Gothic style. It comprises chancel, nave and western tower, once apparently embattled and with pinnacles but now having only a simple parapet. The organ, contained in the west tower, was built by J.E. Bishop in 1845. It was rebuilt in 1898

*St. Margaret's church where Charlie was baptised.*

at a cost of £200. The clock was made in 1821 by John Moore of London. It was renovated in 1912. There are two bells, one of 1714 and one of 1834. The former one came from the Royal Hospital Greenwich and may have been presented to the church by William Hutton. There are also two smaller bells on which the clock strikes the quarters. Burials began in 1833 and the register dates from 1843."

When I visited the church in 2007 it had fallen into disrepair. The doors and windows were boarded up, and the graveyard was in need of urgent attention. Graffiti had been sprayed on the St Margaret's sign, and it was sad to see the old church in such a mess. I'm pleased to report that, a year later, the church grounds were cleared, and the old church may soon be re-opened again for services.

Incidentally Frank Gwyther died in 1891, and in 1903 his widow, Charlotte Elizabeth, sold Ward End House and some land to the Birmingham Corporation. A year later it became Ward End Park.

The Cottages where Charlie was born, were very close to the Park, and I'm sure the Halls spent many hours playing there. In 1906, the Right Honourable Joseph Chamberlain visited the Park to celebrate his seventieth birthday. Large crowds of people turned out to see him – perhaps one of them was Charlie?

There has been some confusion over which was Charlie's first school. We know from later interviews with his brother Frank, that he attended Leigh

*Leigh Road school with its tower.*

Road School and left there around 1913. However, as the school only opened in 1909, his first years in education, were obviously spent somewhere else. For some reason, the local press (recently) claimed that Charlie went to Slade Road School, which opened in 1903.

This seems unlikely, as it is too far from where he lived. From his address it appears that he went to the 'Little Bromwich National School' (called Ward End School, or to the locals, the Church school). At that time most children attended the school that was nearest to their home, and this certainly fits the bill. Logbooks from the school survive from this period.

The entries are fascinating, and they give us an insight into what school was like at this period in time. The school had no means of lighting and was heated by coal.

The first entry is in the year 1863 and reads:

Mary Anne Moore commenced duty as mistress of Little Bromwich National School, January 5th, 1863.

**January 20th**
Logbook brought to the school by Reverend J.F.Green.

**February 2nd – 6th**
School closed, key having been lost.

**March 2nd**
Two boys sent home to be washed.

**July 7th**
I sent back two children this morning who have been at home some time, it having being said they have the itch.

**September 8th**
A wet morning and the chimney smoking badly. I sent them home at 11.15am.

There are only two extracts from when Charlie was at the School. The date is 1905 and they read as follows.

**March 23rd**
Fire Drill. A test was taken this morning and the school was completely emptied in a minute and a half from the time that the whistle was blown.

**October 18th**
Considerable inconvenience is being experienced from the failure of the water supply here as well as from imperfect drains. A pool quite 12ft across collects in playground after heavy rain.

At some point between 1905–1908 the Gwyther cottages were given a street number (580) of Washwood Heath Road. The Hall family eventually moved to a new address at 33 Arley Road, Saltley, Birmingham, which was only a few hundred yards from the cottages, where Charlie was born.

England had come to the end of the Victorian era, and education was now becoming very important. New schools were springing up all over Birmingham (many of which are still standing) and one such school was Leigh Road. Many children were now going to school for the first time, and Charlie, unlike his father, was receiving an education.

On Thursday September 2nd 1909 this is how the Birmingham Daily Mail covered the opening of the school in Leigh Road:

## "NEW SCHOOL AT WASHWOOD HEATH"

## LORD MAYOR ON EDUCATIONAL PROGRESS

*"The Lord Mayor of Birmingham (Alderman, Sir George Kenrick) opened a new school in Leigh Road, Washwood Heath last night. The school will accommodate 1,000 children, and will serve a number of other schools in the district as a centre for manual instruction and the teaching of cookery and laundry. The provision of the school, which has been constructed and equipped on the most approved lines, has involved an outlay of about £12,000, of which £2,200 represents the cost of the site. The opening ceremony was attended by a large number of the inhabitants of the district and by members of the Education Committee and the City Council. Mr G. Bethune Baker presided, and in inviting the Lord Mayor to declare the school open, presented to him on behalf of the members of the Education Committee a metal key embossed in gold, and designed and made at the School of Art.*

*The Lord Mayor in opening the school said in the elementary schools today they were teaching very much what was taught in the grammar schools in Birmingham thirty or forty years ago. (Hear, hear.) The quality of the elementary school teaching was now quite equal to that given in the grammar schools of the period mentioned. It was true it was not the same. With rare exceptions, Latin or French was not taught in the elementary schools, but they were teaching certain subjects that were not taught in the grammar schools of thirty or forty years since. From those grammar schools came many men who today hold high positions in the City Council, or on the Bench, or as manufacturers, and everybody knew that with the education they received they had done very well. There was no reason why those who now attended the elementary schools should not do as well; but as a matter of fact, we had got beyond that stage, for it was now possible for the cleverest of the scholars in the elementary school to go on to the secondary school, which was far in advance of anything available in Birmingham thirty or forty years ago. In visiting an elementary school that day he was astonished to find the large proportion of children who passed through it to the secondary school. If the children could take those positions there was not a great deal the matter with the training given in the elementary schools. He did not wish to say that the top had been reached; there was no top, and never would be a top in this matter, for there was always room for something more and something new. But the great change that had been made was the extension of what was the privilege of the few to be the right of all. (Applause.) He hoped that whatever Birmingham did it would always be determined that its schools should be first, and of the best, and would not allow anyone to say that they had fallen behind the times."*

Apparently the new school was fitted with the 'plenum system' which would guarantee fresh clean air into the classrooms. The air was led into the classrooms through ducts, which opened out under the galleries. It was abstracted through ducts at ceiling height. The school's first headmaster was Mr. T. W. Cooper, who would remain at the school until the end of January 1925. At the end of the first week there were 873 pupils enrolled at Leigh Road.

We believe this is where Charlie first picked up his skills as a carpenter. Incredibly the school organised two outings in 1910. One was to the local Aston Hall (which still stands today) and the second trip was to London. It may have included a certain Charlie Hall.

By 1914 most of the male staff at the school were 'called up' as the First World War had begun.

It has often been said that when Charlie left school, he got a job working with his father. However this is not the case. His father was still working down in the sewers, and we know that Charlie became a carpenter.

Charlie got himself a job working for a local company called The Metropolitan Railway Carriage & Wagon Co. Ltd. This was a very famous Birmingham Company based in Saltley. It later became known as Metro-Cammell and it moved its base to Washwood Heath. It was still making trains until it finally closed in 2005.

The skills Charlie picked up working as a carpenter would prove to be invaluable for the rest of his life.

Past articles and books on Charlie Hall, claim that he joined the Fred Karno Company, and it was here that he first worked with Stan Laurel (then Stan Jefferson). But is this true?

Stan was indeed in Birmingham in 1910 touring with Fred Karno's 'Company of Comedians' and they performed at The Birmingham Empire

*1911 census.*

and Birmingham Hippodrome (Charlie Chaplin was the lead comedian). As Charlie Hall was only 10 years old at the time, it seems highly unlikely that he was part of the company.

There is also a belief that when Charlie left for New York, who should be playing there, but the Fred Karno Company. And it was here that Stan persuaded Charlie to go to Hollywood. This is a nice tale, but unfortunately not true.

We know from the 1911 census that Charlie was working as a paperboy for a local newsagent. So while the Fred Karno Company was touring the US, our Charlie was delivering newspapers!

So why is Charlie always linked with the Fred Karno Company? Charlie himself may have the answer.

In an interview he gave in 1938, he mentions Fred Karno Jr. taking a comedy act on tour in 1924. Charlie claims he was one of the outfit. Perhaps upon seeing the name Fred Karno, people automatically think it is Fred Karno Snr.

A quick check of the records shows that Fred Karno Jr. was working at the Hal Roach Studios (as Charlie says) in 1924. We also know that Charlie and Fred Jr. appeared in at least four comedies together in that year. So we can only presume that this is where the confusion arises.

There is now a gap in our story. The First World War was to run between 1914 and 1918. According to all his family, Charlie did not serve in the Army. What he was doing at this time remains a mystery; none of his family can shed any light on this period.

He may have carried on working at the Metropolitan Railway works, as the company had a very important role, making tanks for the British Army.

*Charlie got a job at The Metropolitan Railway Carriage and Wagon Company. This photograph of the company dates from 1898.*

## Chapter Two

# CHARLIE HEADS FOR THE U.S.

By the end of 1919, Charlie had decided to try a new life for himself across the Atlantic, in the USA. And on the 12th January 1920, Charlie set sail. (Although he claims the departure was delayed for a couple of days). He was on board the S.S. Carmania, which sailed from the port of Liverpool and arrived in America on 24th January.

*A young looking Charlie Hall.*

It was generally thought, that he was on his way to visit his sister Florence. This we now know is incorrect. Florence was still in Birmingham at the time, and did not leave until the following year.

In fact Charlie left England, to take a job working in a canning factory, and we can see from the passenger lists that he was meeting someone called F. T. Briggs.

The passenger records have his last place of residence as Dewsbury, but this is unlikely to be correct. Immediately before him on the passenger list, is a family from Dewsbury called, Hill. So it looks like a simple clerical error.

On the 'List Or Manifest Of Alien Passengers For The United States Immigration Officer At Port Of Arrival', Charlie is number 17. The records show that Charles Hall was 20 years and 3 months old, and under the heading 'Calling or Occupation' he is

*The Carmania, the ship that took Charlie to New York in 1920.*

listed as a Turner. The name and address of his nearest relative is given as his Father, Mr. T. Hall, 33 Arley Road, Saltley, Birmingham. The records also show that Charlie paid for the trip himself and on arrival had $58 in his pocket. His height is listed as 5' 4½" and his eyes were brown. Under the heading 'Whether going to join a relative or friend; and if so, What relative or friend, and his name and complete address,' Charlie doesn't list his sister. The name Pennsylvania Hotel N.Y. City is clearly typed. Above this is a name that is difficult to read. It may be F.T. Briggs, the number 12 is underneath and an address that is difficult to make out.

What is interesting is that Charlie arrived in the US, just as 'Prohibition' had started. Prohibition banned the sale, manufacture and transport of alcohol, and incredibly lasted until 1933.

Charlie liked a drink, and I'm sure he managed to find one amongst the numerous 'speakeasies' that sprung up all over New York.

However working in a canning factory was not for Charlie. He made a momentous decision to leave New York and make his way to Hollywood.

Hollywood at this time was engulfed in various scandals. In 1921 Fatty Arbuckle was accused of assaulting an actress (Virginia Rappe). Although he was innocent, the press had a field day, dwelling on the illegal drinking and 'wild parties' that Hollywood had become known for. In 1922 William Desmond Taylor was found shot dead, and Mabel Normand was the last person to see him alive. The mystery of his death was never solved. Even worse was to follow for Mabel. On 1st January 1924 Mabel and her friend

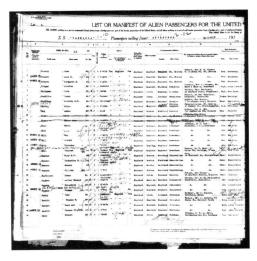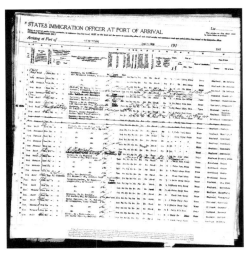

*Record of Charlie's crossing to the US in 1920.*

Edna Purviance were in the house of Courtland S. Dines when he too was murdered. The murderer was Mabel's chauffeur, Joe Kelly (real name Horace Green).

Once again the press had a field day, and various states pulled the showing of Mabel's film 'The Extra Girl'.

Edna Purviance also suffered in that she missed out on appearing in a new film being cast by Charlie Chaplin, called the 'The Gold Rush'.

So this was the Hollywood Charlie had entered, but once in Hollywood, he claimed, *"I walked down towards Sunset Boulevard, and there was my first studio 'Lasky's"*.

Lasky's was known, as the 'Famous Players Lasky Corporation' and would later become Paramount Pictures.

Charlie also claimed that he worked for Mack Sennett, Larry Semon, Cecil B.DeMille and various other studios. As all studios used a lot of extras, this is probably true.

He eventually made his way to the Hal Roach Studios and he would remain with Hal Roach until 1940.

Charlie loved being at the Hal Roach Studios, and claimed that Hal treated all his staff very well.

Charlie stated that at Christmas time, Hal would hand out presents to everyone at the studio. This is born out by Fay Wray who said that Hal gave beautiful beaded bags to all the girls under contract who worked at his studios. The Hal Roach Studios was known as 'The Lot of Fun' and to Charlie it certainly was.

## Chapter Three

# WHAT WAS CHARLIE'S FIRST FILM?

So what was Charlie Hall's first film? Even now it is difficult to pin down. In his book 'The Laurel and Hardy Stock Company', Leo Brooks claims it is 'The Soilers'. He writes: "Joe Collum and the others on the Roach lot took a shine to the fiesty, cocky little Englishman. In November of 1923, Charlie was working part-time on the lot as a carpenter and living in lodgings about four blocks from the studio. Stan (Laurel) and Jimmy Finlayson were working on a two-reeler called 'The Soilers'. They were short a cast member, so Charlie was pressed into service. According to Collum, while Charlie and Stan would later become life long friends, there was no indication of this friendship at this early date."

The above sounds very convincing, but was Charlie in this film? The answer would appear to be, no!

The film 'The Soilers' was filmed in August/September 1923. We know Charlie appeared in the 1923 film 'Mother's Joy' (as a houseguest) which incidentally was filmed just nine days after 'The Soilers'.

Both of the above films included Stan Jefferson (Laurel) and his wife Mae. It later turned out that Stan and Mae were not in fact married (but that is another story). It was Mae who claimed she persuaded Stan to change his name to Laurel. Stan Jefferson was superstitious and he realised that his name had 13 letters in it. Mae was flicking through a magazine and came across a roman wearing a laurel wreath on his head. She suggested the name Laurel to Stan and he approved of it.

Back to Charlie's first film, and to complicate matters further the IMDB (Internet Movie Data Base) lists the 1921 silent movie 'The Janitor' as Charlie's first film. This film starred Billy Franey. This is however incorrect. Charlie Hall is not in 'The Janitor'.

So until we have further evidence, we will say Charlie Hall's first known film is 'Mother's Joy'.

1924 saw Charlie appear in various films with Stan Laurel at the Hal Roach Studios.

These included 'Smithy', 'Postage Due', 'Zeb Vs Paprika' and 'Near Dublin'. He also appeared with Charley Chase, Will Rogers and Glenn Tryon.

In 1925 Charlie claimed he was an extra in Charlie Chaplin's classic film 'The Gold Rush' and there is no reason to doubt this, although no footage of him can be found.

Over the next two years he would appear in many films at the Hal Roach Studios, which also included James Finlayson and 'Our Gang'. James Finlayson, Stan Laurel and Charlie all appeared in the 1927 'Our Gang' film 'Seeing the world'. We presume that Charlie was still working as a carpenter on site, as his parts in the above films were only small.

Whilst at the Hal Roach Studios, Charlie made many friends, and some of them such as Edgar Kennedy and George Stevens would play a large part in his life.

*Chapter Four*

# CHARLIE'S EARLY SILENT FILMS

Charlie's appearances in Laurel and Hardy's silent films were varied, to say the least. Blink and you will miss him in some films, but he would feature prominently in others. In fact you could say that about all Charlie Hall's films! But as we shall see, he was to make a lasting impression in some of the screen's most famous films of all time.

Hal Roach described Charlie as 'The Little Menace', and our 'Little Menace' would go on to menace Laurel and Hardy many times over the next few years.

Some of the films were made, but not released until months later, so I will put them in the order they were made.

**Love 'Em And Weep**

In April 1927 (released in June) Charlie Hall appeared in his first Laurel and Hardy film called 'Love 'Em And Weep'. Charlie has a small scene as the butler alongside James Finlayson.

In this film businessman Titus Tillsbury (James Finlayson) asks Stan to keep an old flame (Mae Busch) away from an important dinner party he is giving. This film was later remade as a talkie, 'Chickens Come Home' and James Finlayson would take Charlie's part as the butler.

It is fitting that Charlie's first Laurel and Hardy film should be with Mae Busch and James Finlayson. In years to come, the Sons of the Desert (the worldwide Laurel and Hardy Appreciation Society) would toast Charlie, Mae and James Finlayson at all their tent meetings (More about the Sons of the Desert later).

*Charlie as the butler, in the first of his film appearances with Laurel and Hardy. This is the 1927 film Love 'Em And Weep.*

## With Love and Hisses

Brad Farrell only discovered Charlie Hall's brief walk-on appearance in this film while he was watching the film in 2007. Early on in the film, Charlie can be seen on the left of the screen dressed as a soldier.

Although still not officially a team, in this film we can see the makings of Laurel and Hardy. Stan and Ollie are appearing together, Ollie as the Army Sergeant giving orders to a dim-witted Private Stan.

## Sugar Daddies

Charlie's part in the next Laurel and Hardy film is just as brief. In 'Sugar Daddies', Lawyer Stan and Butler Ollie help a millionaire with his romantic entanglements (the millionaire is played by James Finlayson).

Charlie has a part as an extra standing by the hotel lift.

## The Second Hundred Years

'The Second Hundred Years', is widely regarded as Laurel and Hardy's first film together as a team (partly credited to Leo McCarey).

Laurel and Hardy escape jail by turning their striped uniforms inside-out and posing as painters. Charlie's part as a convict is difficult to find. But if you look closely, he is on the far left on the line of convicts.

Stan Laurel had his head shaved for his role in this film, and when he started growing his hair again, he found that it kept sticking up. It resulted in the Stan Laurel look we know today – hair sticking up at the front, which he would pull his fingers through as he scratched his head.

Charlie Hall claims he was responsible for this. Here is his version of events:

*"The last picture of the series that Hal Roach made was a prison story, and both Babe and Stan had their hair shaved off. I remember that event well, because I was the barber and I have never seen less faith in a tonsorial artist in my life.*

*Just after that the studios closed down for six weeks, not that they had any connection with my activities as a barber, and Stan went home for the first time since 1910.*

*On his return Hal had a new story ready for him and Babe, but to Stan's profound horror he found that his hair was in the intermediate stage of growing, and would not stick down whatever was done to it. He plastered it with cream. He ladled oil on it, but it still stuck straight up. Stan went to Hal with his troubles. This Stan in distress was the identical Stan in distress that you now know in pictures, and Hal just roared with laughter. When he got over his first paroxysms he said:*

*'If it's funny to me it's funny to others.' And Hal was right. It gave Stan Laurel something that he lacked. It gave him a definite personality of his own, and this picture that I mentioned before, 'The Battle of the Century' really put Laurel and Hardy on the map".*

## The Call of the Cuckoo

The 'Call of the Cuckoo' is a Max Davidson comedy made for Hal Roach, featuring Laurel and Hardy. This film has Max Davidson living next door to a school for radio announcers. These are Stan Laurel, Oliver Hardy, James Finlayson and Charley Chase, who appear to be acting 'Cuckoo'.

It starts with Oliver Hardy wheeling in Charlie Hall like a wheelbarrow. These four great silent clowns then line up in front of Charlie (who is wearing a paper hat) with brooms over their shoulders. Charlie turns around and says "Quick march" at which point, they all hit Charlie over the head with their brooms.

Charlie Hall was now working with some of the very best comedians of all time. And the year was to end with Charlie playing a pie delivery man in one of Laurel and Hardy's most famous silent films 'The Battle of the Century'.

Not only that, but Charlie would have two parts in the film.

## The Battle of the Century

'The Battle of the Century' is one of the most famous silent comedy shorts of all time. It is one of the films that Laurel and Hardy will always be associated with, as it contains the famous pie fight!

It was released in December 1927 and was based on 'The Fight of the Century' between the two great heavyweight boxers of that era, Gene Tunney and Jack Dempsey. Stan Laurel plays the part of a prizefighter with Babe as his manager. There is a hilarious fight sequence between Stan and Noah Young, in which Stan gets knocked out.

During the fight scene we see Charlie Hall for the first time in this film. He is at the ringside dressed in a pin stripe suit, a Bowler Hat, and has a false moustache. At one point he gets a bit carried away and knocks the microphone over.

When the fight is over, Ollie decides to buy an accident policy on Stan. To help Stan have an accident he drops a banana skin in his path. However it's the pieman Charlie Hall who slips on the skin, and Charlie takes his revenge by letting Oliver Hardy have one of his pies flush in the face. This is the start of the biggest pie fight the silent screen had ever seen. Over 3,000 pies (ordered from the Los Angeles Pie Company) were thrown and every one of them made their mark.

Alas not all of this film has survived. Fortunately for us the classic pie fight sequence has. This is, you could say, the first appearance of Charlie as 'The Little Menace'. And Charlie himself claims it was Stan Laurel who came up with the idea. Until then the bad guy had always been a big man (known as a heavy) but Charlie was only 5ft 4 in. This made his 'spats' with Laurel and Hardy more hilarious.

Again we can hear Charlie's own version of events:

*"I played the pie man. Stan and Babe were walking past a pie shop. Babe was peeling a banana, and threw the skin in the doorway just as I came out with a trayful of pies. Of course down I went. Babe saw me, and handed the banana to Stan, implicating him as the culprit.*

*I got up and walked slowly up to Stan, and it was here that we changed our technique, or rather Stan changed it for us, for it was his idea.*

*Up to then the 'heavy' had always been a big man, and the mess he made of the small comic was nobody's business. But I was only 5ft 4in, and in this scene I just went up to Babe and gently twisted his nose, put my finger in his eye, and flipped him in the Adam's apple.*

*As I walked away to pick up my tray Stan blew his nose, and as I bent over my tray I heard the unmistakable raspberry. Thinking it was Babe, I picked up a pie and let him have it full in the face. Babe still stood there just looking vacant. Stan said to Babe: 'Are you going to let him get away with that?' At the same time picking up a pie and handing it to Babe to throw at me. Babe threw it and as I ducked the pie landed on the pavement.*

*\*Thelma Todd, then a stock girl, came along, slipped on the pie and fell right on it. When she got up all you could see was a grease spot on the pavement where the pie had been, and it was obvious from her antics that the pie was sticking to her – anatomy.*

*With a look of rage she picked up a pie and slammed it at Stan, but missed and hit a policeman. That started it, and before we knew where we were there were 200 people all throwing pies. We threw 5000 pies in that scene. Was it a wow? It made Laurel and Hardy.*

*It was the old stuff in a new setting. The Laurel and Hardy team has thrown thousands more pies and made thousands more laugh. Honest to goodness slapstick is welcomed by the general public.*

*When I tell you that Hal Roach is the owner of the world's greatest fun factory I can find no more truthful or adequate description of that amazing laughter-raising organisation."*

*\*Charlie is mistaken. It is not Thelma Todd, who slips on the pie, but Anita Garvin. And his claim of 5000 pies thrown is a slight exaggeration.

It's incredible to think that just seven years after leaving Birmingham, Charlie Hall would throw the first pie in one of the most famous scenes in comedy history!

If that wasn't enough, Charlie also had an important part in the 1927 Buster Keaton film 'College'.

In this film Buster Keaton gives a speech about how books are better than sports (much to the annoyance of his girlfriend) so to try and win her back he enrols at a college to learn more about sports.

After failing at quite a few sports, Buster explains his predicament to a sympathetic Dean. The Dean in turn makes Buster coxswain of the boat crew, much to the disgust of the team coach.

It's here we see Charlie for the first time in the film, as the coach gives the crew the news that Buster is to be the coxswain. Charlie is the original coxswain and he is none too pleased. But it is the Dean's orders, unless something happens to Buster. On the day of the race Charlie says to the coach: "Hey coach, nothing has happened to Mama's boy!" The coach then

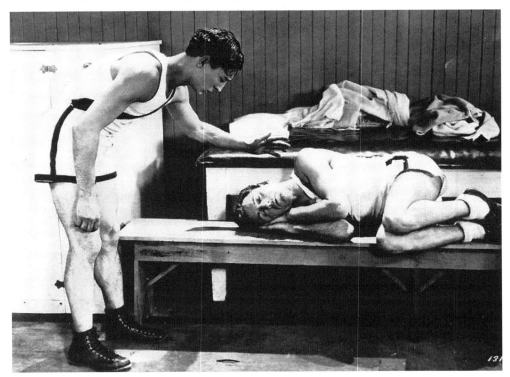

*Charlie takes a nap in Buster Keaton's 'College'.*

hands Charlie two cups of tea, and he puts some powder in one of them. Of course the cups get changed, and Charlie ends up drinking the wrong tea.

The scene then switches to the locker room with Charlie and Buster sitting side by side. Charlie starts to yawn and he eventually curls up on the bench and falls asleep. Buster tries in vain to wake him and carries a very limp Charlie Hall outside and drops him at the coach's feet. Buster becomes the coxswain and wins the race for the college and he wins back his girlfriend. So I think it is fair to say that 1927 was a very good year for Charlie Hall.

**Leave 'Em Laughing**
Charlie's next film with Laurel and Hardy was 'Leave 'Em Laughing.' Today the film is famous for the fact that the TV series 'Friends' had a poster of it showing very prominently on the wall.

Stan has toothache and has tried several attempts to pull the tooth out, including tying a piece of string around the tooth and the doorknob.

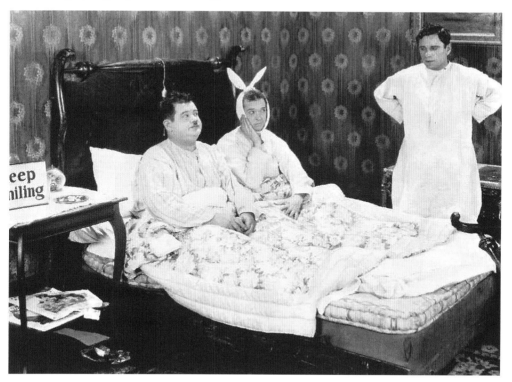

*Charlie in 'Leave 'Em Laughing', asking Stand and Ollie to keep the noise down.*

Charlie Hall (the landlord) enters the room in his nightshirt and tells the boys to keep the noise down.

As Charlie is leaving the room, Stan kicks Charlie up the rear. Charlie returns and kicks Ollie. Ollie kicks Charlie. Eventually Stan punches Charlie very comically in the face. With this, Charlie appears as if he is drunk on his feet, and staggers out of the room. He somehow manages to wave to Stan and finally walks backward out of shot.

This, as we will find out, is a typical meeting between Stan, Ollie and Charlie.

**Your Darn Tootin'**

1928, and in 'Your Darn Tootin' Laurel and Hardy are musicians in a band. Charlie's part in this film is very small. You can spot him sitting next to Oliver Hardy, as one of the bandstand musicians.

**Should Married Men Go Home?**

A few months later, Charlie appears in his 9th film with Laurel and Hardy, 'Should Married Men Go Home?'

Stan and Babe only have fifteen cents to buy four sodas. Charlie plays the part of the Soda Jerk who is serving them. This sequence would later be reworked in the film 'Men 'O War', and once again, Charlie's part would be played by James Finlayson.

**Two Tars**

The last film Charlie made with Laurel and Hardy in this year was the wonderful 'Two Tars'.

Stan and Ollie are sailors who encounter two girls having trouble getting bubblegum out of a machine. Of course they go over to help. Ollie accidentally spills the bubblegum all over the pavement. This causes Stan and the girls to run back to the car leaving Ollie to pick up the gum.

Charlie comes out of the shop and slaps Ollie's hands and gum falls out of them. He then presses Ollie's stomach, lifts up his sweater and more gum balls fall out. With this he punches Ollie in the stomach and flicks him on his behind. Stan sees what is going on and returns. There is a great caption that comes up and it reads: "You're flirtin' with death, son".

Stan tries to hit Charlie but keeps slipping on the gum. This leads to Charlie punching him in the face. The two girls now enter the scene and they tell Stan and Ollie to wait in the car. One of the girls kicks Charlie in the shin and rustles his hair.

With this they leave Charlie and walk back to the car. Charlie then leans on a table, which collapses to the floor. The 'Little Menace' has tangled with the Boys again, and this time Charlie's part in the film lasted for over two minutes.

The silent films were coming to an end. And in the year 1929 Laurel and Hardy began making 'Talkies'. Al Jolson appeared in Warner Brothers first feature talkie, 'The Jazz Singer', in October 1927 and it caused a sensation. Now everybody wanted to hear their favourite film stars speak. For Stan Laurel and Oliver Norvell Hardy this wouldn't be a problem, although Stan was a bit concerned about his voice. He didn't have to worry. As for Ollie, the new sound pictures would give him a chance to show off his wonderful singing voice, as well as his beautiful southern accent. He was very proud of his southern roots, and now both these brilliant clowns would use sound to their advantage.

But for many silent film stars of the day, it was the end of their careers. However, Stan and Ollie were not finished with silent films just yet, and they would go on to make quite a few more.

*Charlie as the shopkeeper in the 1928 film 'Two Tars'.*

*Charlie as a pickpocket in the 1928 film 'The Butter and Egg Man'.*

**Wrong Again**
A millionaire has lost a painting called 'Blue Boy'. Stan and Babe believe that it is a horse called 'Blue Boy' that is missing and take the horse to the millionaire.

Charlie appears at the end of the film in a white hat, just as a policeman confiscates a gun from the millionaire. "This man almost blew my brains out" the caption reads. The policeman turns around to reveal he has been shot in the backside!

**That's My Wife**
His brief appearance in this film is as a waiter. A drunk asks him for a bowl of soup to take out. Charlie can then be spotted as he draws back the curtains and reveals Oliver Hardy trying to get a necklace out of the back of Stan's dress. Stan is dressed as a woman to try to convince Ollie's uncle that he is happily married, so he can claim his inheritance.

*A blackened Charlie in the 1928 film 'Lady Be Good'.*

## Big Business

As I've mentioned, Laurel and Hardy were not quite finished with silent films. And in 1928, they began work on what I believe is one of the greatest silent comedy shorts of all time 'Big Business'.

Laurel and Hardy are selling Christmas trees, when they approach the house of James Finlayson. Although it looks like Laurel and Hardy are selling Christmas trees in summer, this film was actually filmed in December. Finlayson doesn't want to buy a Christmas tree, but Stan and Babe's perseverance leads to an altercation, which gets completely out of hand. In a tit for tat exchange, Laurel and Hardy set about destroying James Finlayson's house, as Fin systematically destroys their car.

Never has such destruction been done to a property or a car in the name of comedy. Charlie can be seen amongst the crowd of people watching this incredible spectacle take place. He is wearing a white hat with a black rim around it, and is easily recognisable.

Although Charlie only has the part of an extra, to be associated with this film is still a wonderful achievement.

## Double Whoopee

This film was shot in 1929. As doorman and footman at a high-class hotel, Laurel and Hardy manage to upset a number of the guests. The film co-starred the very beautiful Jean Harlow (who went on to be known as 'The Platinum Blonde'). She would also go on to fame in Howard Hughes's World War 1 epic 'Hell's Angels', plus various films with Clark Gable. Jean Harlow tragically died at the early age of 26 (of uremic poisoning) on June 7th 1937.

Yet again 'Double Whoopee' pits Charlie against the Boys. Ollie (the doorman) is standing outside the hotel and cannot resist blowing his whistle that is attached to his uniform. Upon hearing the whistle Charlie appears driving a taxi.

*Jean Harlow.*

*Charlie's in trouble again. This time in the film 'Double Whoopee'.*

"It blew" the caption reads as Ollie tries to cover his embarrassment at blowing the whistle.

Charlie reacts angrily. "Well don't let it blew again. Now I've got to drive clear round the block."

Later in the film Stan and Ollie are standing outside the hotel and this time it is Stan who blows the whistle on Ollie's uniform.

Charlie appears again, and this time he gets out of the taxi. "You blew it again, sweetheart" the caption reads.

Ollie points the finger at Stan. "He's too dumb to blow it" is Charlie's next caption.

Charlie then pulls the whistle off Ollie's uniform, throws it to the ground and proceeds to tread on it, squashing it under his foot. He then pulls out Ollie's handkerchief and tears it in two. At this point Stan has just bent down and he thinks he has split his trousers.

Still not finished, Charlie then removes Ollie's cap and rips the peak off it, before replacing it on Ollie's head.

Stan decides to join in, and he pulls the peak on Charlie's cap down his face and under his chin. It now looks like Charlie has a beard.

Ollie finds this very funny and bursts out laughing.

Charlie turns his attention back to Ollie, and pulls a button off his coat. A policeman (played by Tiny Sandford) arrives on the scene and Charlie pulls a button off his uniform as well.

The policeman tries to throttle Charlie, but he ducks, and he grabs Stan by the throat instead.

This gives Charlie a chance to escape and he runs to his taxi and drives off, with the policeman in hot pursuit.

A little later in the film Charlie appears again as he rushes into the hotel, with the policeman not far behind.

## Bacon Grabbers

In this film we find Stan and Babe working for the Sheriff's Office, as they attempt to re-possess a radio. Once again it was to include Jean Harlow.

Stan and Ollie come out of the office and get in their car. They move a few inches forward and manage to hit a truck, which is parked directly in front of them. The truck, as you can probably guess, is driven by Charlie Hall.

Ollie gets out of the car to inspect the damage, and water from their car radiator shoots out over his backside. Charlie laughs and the caption reads: "It could 'a' been worse. You might 'a' been drivin' an automobile".

Charlie drives off and his part in the film is complete.

1929 was another good year for Charlie. He appeared in some of the first 'Our Gang' and Charley Chase talkies, as well as in one of famous silent film comedian Harry Langdon's first, 'Skirt Shy' all for Hal Roach Studios.

The year was now coming to an end, and Charlie appeared in the last silent film Laurel and Hardy ever made, called 'Angora Love'.

## Angora Love

Stan and Ollie are lumbered with a goat, which they take back to their boarding house. The boys are washing the goat when Charlie (in his dressing gown) knocks on their door. Laurel and Hardy think it is the landlord and Ollie takes the goat out of the tub and pushes Stan's head in the tub instead.

"Pardon me, wrong room," says Charlie and he leaves. He re-enters the room just as Stan throws the contents of the tub at landlord Edgar Kennedy, but it misses and hits Charlie in the face. Charlie leaves the room but returns with a bucket of water, which he in turn throws over Edgar Kennedy.

A lot of gags in this film would later be used in 'Laughing Gravy' although, this time of course, Charlie would play the landlord.

Laurel and Hardy would now move onto making 'talkies'. Charlie would move on with them, and he would feature in many of their films, even taking the lead roles in a few of them. Not bad for a 'chippy' from Ward End, Birmingham.

## Chapter Five

# THE GREAT STARS OF YESTERYEAR

So just a few years after leaving Birmingham, Charlie was working with some of the great names of the silent screen. So who where these people he worked with? Let's start with Stan Laurel.

### Stan Laurel

I believe that Stan Laurel was probably the funniest person who has ever lived. A true genius of comedy and comedic timing bettered by no one. It is impossible not to laugh when Stan has done something wrong, or he starts to cry, or he starts scratching his head. Yet although in the films it appears Stan had little or no sense, in real life he was the driving force behind the team of Laurel and Hardy.

He was born Arthur Stanley Jefferson on June 16th 1890 in Ulverston, England. His father (known as A.J.) owned various theatres throughout the north of England and Scotland. Stan made his debut at the age of 16 at the Britannia Theatre, Glasgow. The theatre still stands (now known as The Panopticon) and it is hoped that sufficient funds can be raised to bring this marvellous old theatre back to its former glory.

In 1909 Stan joined the famous Fred Karno troupe that toured the UK, and in 1910 they set off to the USA with a certain Charlie Chaplin as lead comedian, (Stan was Charlie's understudy).

Chaplin soon became an international star, and Stan Laurel was destined to follow. Around 1920/21 Stan appeared in a film called 'The Lucky Dog' with a certain Oliver Hardy, although their teaming was still a few years off. Eventually they got together and made the world laugh in over 100 films.

Stan passed away on February 23rd 1965.

### Oliver Hardy

He was born Norvell Hardy in Harlem, Georgia, on January 18th 1892. His father (who was called Oliver) passed away when Norvell was only 10 months old. His mother ran a Hotel in nearby Madison and it was here that he used to observe people as they came and went.

*Laurel and Hardy.*

He had a beautiful singing voice, and at one stage it looked like he would make this his career. He would occasionally sing in Laurel and Hardy films and it always enhanced the film.

By 1910 he began running the first movie theatre in Milledgeville, Georgia. It was while watching these silent films, that Hardy decided this is what he would like to do. In 1913 he made his way to Jacksonville, Florida and, over the next few years made over 100 comedies for the Lubin and Vim companies.

It was here that he took his father's name, Oliver. However he was very proud of his own name, so in the Laurel and Hardy films, he would always introduce himself as "Oliver Norvell Hardy".

In his personal life he was known as 'Babe' Hardy, a nickname that he was given by an Italian barber, who applied talc to Oliver's cheeks and would say to him, "nice-a-baby, nice-a-baby". This soon shortened to Babe, and the name was to remain with him all his life.

Oliver Hardy was the perfect partner for Stan. On screen, he was a very funny man. When he looks directly into the camera, the audience shares his feelings. He is famous for wiggling his tie, and his boyish mannerisms suited the team perfectly. For a big man, Oliver Hardy was very light on his feet, which was another asset to this great comedy team.

And his saying, "Here's another nice mess you've got me into", is still as well known today as it has always been.

He passed away on 7th August 1957.

### James Finlayson

Known on the Hal Roach lot as Jimmy, but to all Laurel and Hardy fans worldwide, he is known as Fin. He is probably the best known and best loved of the entire Laurel and Hardy co-stars. With his bald head and false moustache, he is easily recognisable.

He was the master of the 'Double-take' and Stan Laurel would say of him, "He would only have to raise his eyebrow to make me laugh."

His catch phrase "Doh!" has been adopted by Homer Simpson, of The Simpsons fame.

He was born in Larbert, NR Falkirk, Scotland on August 27th 1887. After touring the British Music Halls, he moved to the USA to star in the 1912 show 'Bunty Pulls the Strings'. He made various films for other studios including Mack Sennett, before moving to the Hal Roach Studios. He would go on to appear in 33 Laurel and Hardy comedies.

He died on October 9th 1953. *James Finlayson.*

### Buster Keaton

Joseph Frank 'Buster' Keaton was born on the 4th October 1895 in Piqua, Kansas, USA. He is probably best known for his silent films and his trademark deadpan expression, earning him the nickname 'The Great Stone Face'.

The legendary magician Harry Houdini supposedly gave him the nickname 'Buster'. Apparently he fell down a flight of stairs and to Houdini's amazement remained unharmed. "Some Buster", Houdini said, and the name stuck.

Keaton appeared in many comedies with his good friend Roscoe 'Fatty' Arbuckle.

He would become as famous as Harold Lloyd and Charlie Chaplin, thanks to his superb 1924 silent film 'The Navigator'. His 1927 film 'The General' is today classed as a masterpiece, but at the time, it made a loss at the Box Office.

Keaton gradually slipped out of the public's notice, but the advent of TV saw this comedy genius's work back in vogue. He made live TV appearances, where the audiences would once again laugh out loud at his antics. Fittingly he was back, and the movie world mourned his death on 1st February 1966.

## Mae Busch

Annie Mae Busch was born on 18th June 1891, in Melbourne, Australia. Her family moved to the US around 1900. Mae was placed in St. Elizabeth Convent, New Jersey, while it's thought her parents joined the vaudeville

*Mae Busch stars as Charlie Hall's wife in the film 'Tit For Tat'.*

circuit. Mae left the convent in 1905. In later years Mae would give a different account of her early life, and she gave her date of birth as 1897.

Her earliest known films are 'The Agitator' (1912) and 'The Water Nymph' (1912).

She worked for Keystone and was said to be the 'other woman' in a scandal involving Mack Sennett and his then fiancée Mabel Normand.

In 1927 Mae Busch took a part in her first film with Laurel and Hardy called 'Love 'Em and Weep'. In all she was to appear in 13 of the Laurel and Hardy movies, making her presence felt as Charlie Hall's wife in 'Them Thar Hills' and the follow up 'Tit for Tat'.

She died on April 19th 1946 at the Motion Picture and Television Country Home and Hospital, Encino, California at the age of 54. Incredibly her ashes were left unclaimed until the 1970s, when members of the Way out West Tent of California paid to have her finally laid to rest. Mae's ashes are now at the Chapel of the Pines, Los Angeles, California. She also has a star on the Hollywood Walk of Fame: Mae's star is at 7047 Hollywood Boulevard.

## Thelma Todd

Thelma Todd was born on July 29 1905 in Lawrence, Massachusetts, a small town within three miles of the New Hampshire State line.

She began entering beauty competitions in her early teens, and in 1925 she entered and won the 'Miss Massachusetts' beauty competition. She was spotted and moved to Hollywood to make films. Thelma signed for the Hal Roach Studios and appeared with such stars as Harry Langdon, Charley Chase and of course Laurel and Hardy. She has a superb scene with Stan Laurel in the 1930 film 'Another Fine Mess'.

In 1931 Hal Roach gave Thelma her own series with Zasu Pitts and later Patsy Kelly.

She would also appear in the Marx Brothers films 'Monkey Business' and 'Horse Feathers'.

Her last film was with Laurel and Hardy in 1935 called 'The Bohemian Girl'. However, most of her part was cut from the picture, as the terrible news came through that Thelma Todd had died.

Thelma had a very busy social life and appeared to mix with the wrong crowd.

On the morning of December 16 1935, Thelma Todd was found dead in her car inside the garage of Jewel Carmen. She had suffered facial injuries and was found slumped over the steering wheel. Even today her death remains a mystery. Officially she died of carbon monoxide poisoning.

However, many people believe she was murdered. There have been plenty of candidates as to who the murderer was. Some say the New York gangster "Lucky Luciano" ordered it. Others claim it was her violent ex husband Pat DeCicco, or her on/off boyfriend Roland West. There have been many theories on who killed Thelma Todd, but perhaps we will never know.

## Bobby Dunn

Robert V. Dunn was born on 28th August 1890 in Milwaukee, Wisconsin, USA. Bobby lost one of his eyes in a stunt that went wrong. He fell into a barrel of water, and unfortunately caught his eye on a floating matchstick. He took to wearing a glass eye, which gave him a somewhat cross-eyed appearance. Charlie claims it was Bobby who gave him an introduction into films. He featured in several Laurel and Hardy comedies, notably as the shoplifter in 'Tit for Tat'. This was also one of Charlie's most prominent roles with Laurel and Hardy. Bobby Dunn died on 24th March 1937.

## Charley Chase

Charles Joseph Parrott was born on 20th October 1893 in Baltimore, Maryland, USA.

Charley began working in Mack Sennett's Keystone comedies, finally moving to Hal Roach in 1920.

He was the older brother of James Parrott who also worked at the Hal Roach Studios, first as a comedian and then as a director.

In 1923 he was to star in his own series under his new name Charley Chase. He was the master of comedy embarrassment, and he had a fine singing voice, which he displayed from time to time.

Charley Chase was responsible for bringing Oliver Hardy to the Roach studio, having directed and acted with him years before.

His most prominent appearance in a Laurel and Hardy film was 'Sons of the Desert' in 1933. Unfortunately Hal Roach decided to let Charley go in 1936.

He moved to Columbia a year later, where once again he appeared in his own two-reel comedies, (as well as directing The Three Stooges).

Sadly, Charley was an alcoholic, and the death of his younger brother (James) in 1939 left him devastated. James became involved with drugs and it is said that Charley refused to give him money to buy them.

Charley felt responsible for Jimmy's death and began to drink even more heavily. He was to die of a heart attack just months later in 1940. He was only 46 years old.

## Edgar Kennedy

Edgar Livingston Kennedy was born on 26th April 1890, in Monterey County, California, USA.

He was known as the master of the 'slow burn'; whereby he would run his left hand down from his head, slowly across his face in an attempt to hold his temper.

He was a Keystone Cop for Mack Sennett and it is rumoured that he once fought world heavy weight champion Jack Dempsey. There is some truth in this rumour as Edgar Kennedy was indeed a boxer for a short time, and appeared in the 1920 film 'Daredevil Jack', with Jack Dempsey.

He appeared in and directed films for Laurel and Hardy at the Hal Roach Studios before leaving to join RKO.

At RKO he starred in the long running 'Average Man' series, which ran for seventeen years.

He also appeared in 'Duck Soup' with the Marx Brothers.

He died on November 9th 1948 aged 58 of throat cancer.

## Mabel Normand

Mabel Ethelreid Normand was born on November 9, 1892 in New Brighton, Staten Island, USA.

She worked for D.W.Griffith's Biograph Company, and it was here that she met Mack Sennett. Mack took Mabel with him when he opened the Keystone Studios in 1912.

At Keystone she directed and worked with Charlie Chaplin, and appeared in films with Roscoe 'Fatty' Arbuckle.

The story of the Mack and Mabel 'on-off romance' would run and run. Whether they were ever an item is still a matter of conjecture.
As mentioned earlier in this book, Mabel's short life was littered with scandals.

In 1926 she married Lew Cody, and joined the Hal Roach Studios. At one point she was romantically linked with Charlie Hall.

She died of tuberculosis at the young age of 34.

## Hal Roach

Harry Eugene Roach was born on 14th January 1892 in Elmira, New York. Arriving in Hollywood he found work as an extra in films and it was here he first met Harold Lloyd.

He received a small inheritance and began making films under the name Rolin ('Ro' for Roach and 'lin' for his partner Dan Linthicum). Harold

Lloyd joined him and the 'Lonesome Luke' character was born. Harold then donned a pair of glasses for his new character and this proved to be very successful.

Hal bought out his partner and the Hal Roach Studios were born.

As well as Laurel and Hardy, Hal Roach was responsible for many other comedy series. 'Our Gang', Charley Chase, and Todd and Pitts just to name few.

Hal Roach lived to the grand old age of 100 years. He once said that he was more famous for being 100 years old than for making all those movies. He gave many interviews during his later years, and I had the pleasure of meeting him at a Laurel and Hardy convention, held in Las Vegas in July 1992.

He told an audience that he was going to visit a strip club later that evening! He died a few months later on 2nd November 1992 (I don't think the above visit was related!).

The wonderful Hal Roach Studios were closed in 1961 and all that remains now is a plaque showing where it once stood.

*Chapter Six*

# CHARLIE SPEAKS

We can only imagine the excitement of going to watch 'talking pictures' for the very first time. Here in his own words, is Charlie's take on the new phenomenon.

*"At that time an event occurred that hit Hollywood as it had not been hit before or since.*

*Warner Bros. were up against it. It was a case of sink or swim, but they had in their hands an amazing surprise. They had a process for talking pictures and put their last pocketful of dough into the production. It was featuring Al Jolson and it was called the 'Jazz Singer'.*

*Everybody in Hollywood predicted a dire flop and the extinction of Warners. Experts said it was terrible, awfully slow, too much talking and you could not hear the words. Executives went around saying, 'Well, believe me when I say that I couldn't make out anything of what they were saying except a word here and there. They'll have to put on sub-titles and try to save a bit from the wreck'.*

*What a wreck it was! Just as Hollywood had unanimously and emphatically said No to the talkies the Public said Yes. That film coined a fortune and led to Al Jolson's greater triumph.*

*The talkies then started a headlong panic in Hollywood. Reputations fell over night. Plans were scrapped in the studios and productions abandoned when the fact that the Talkies had come to stay was realised.*

*It was at once discovered that sound helped Laurel and Hardy. They were to be two of the lucky ones, for stars were now on one side of the fence or the other. There was no half way.*

*When I punched Babe on the nose or kicked him on the shins it got more laughs when the audience heard a big 'Ouch' with a funny noise on the striking of the blow, that a gong effect in the orchestra had done.*

*When you look back on silent films in those days it's almost fantastic. Without a word being heard, all those thousands of stories and short films unfolded themselves, and audiences left the theatres as satisfied with their evening's pleasure as now, when productions costing anything from £40,000 to £500,000 are put in front of them."*

## Berth Marks

Charlie Hall's first appearance in a Laurel and Hardy sound film was 'Berth Marks', and yet ironically Charlie doesn't speak!

Laurel and Hardy cause mayhem on an overnight train journey. At one point in the film, Stan walks into a carriage on the train and a woman (who is getting undressed) screams.

Charlie comes out of the same carriage, sees a man who he thinks has made his wife scream, and proceeds to rip the back of his jacket from the bottom to the top. The man (Harry Bernard) doesn't see that it is Charlie who has ripped his jacket, and he stands behind someone washing their hands (Baldwin Cooke). He mistakenly thinks this is the person who has ripped his jacket, so exacts revenge by ripping his jacket in the same manner. As in 'The Battle of the Century', where Charlie started the famous pie fight, in this film he starts a frenzy of ripped jackets and clothes, which spreads all over the train. At the end of the film, the conductor enters the melee. The passengers rip his uniform and it ends up in shreds.

Charlie also appears in the Spanish version of this film, called 'Noche De Duendes' which incorporates 'The Laurel and Hardy Murder Case'. In this version, Ollie falls over a double bass into Charlie's carriage. This time we get quite a glimpse of Charlie's wife getting undressed. The film then proceeds as in 'Berth Marks', with Charlie ripping the jacket of the guy standing outside his carriage.

Hal Roach had the idea that to further popularise Laurel and Hardy, their films would be made into Spanish, German and French. Stan and Babe would learn their words phonetically, although the studio would use foreign speaking actors and actresses, to play varying roles.

However this practice didn't last too long, as it became too expensive, and according to Hal Roach, MGM stopped it because foreign audiences expected all the MGM films to be remade like that too.

## Men O' War

Charlie Hall would now speak his first lines in a Laurel and Hardy film, and the film was called 'Men O' War'.

In this film, Laurel and Hardy are sailors on leave, enjoying a day out in the park. After attempting to buy four sodas for fifteen cents (for two girls they are trying to impress) they eventually hire a rowing boat with disastrous results.

After various attempts to leave their moorings, Stan and Ollie find themselves standing up in a boat trying to swap oars, when Charlie rows backwards into their boat. We now hear Charlie Hall's voice for the first time in a Laurel and Hardy film. And fittingly he's having a go at the Boys, even though it's his fault.

"What are trying to do, you big fat oaf! Bumping into my boat. Dumb-bell."

Stan bends down and scoops some water into his hat and throws it in Charlie's face. Ollie laughs. Charlie takes off Ollie's hat fills it with water and does the same to him. Once again the tit for tat has started.

Ollie now picks up a cushion from his boat and hits Charlie over the head with it. Charlie picks up his cushion and does the same to Ollie. Stan joins in, and he hits Charlie on the head with a cushion.

Ollie now takes Charlie's oar, breaks it in two and hands it back to him. Stan then pushes Charlie into the lake. Charlie manages to climb into Laurel and Hardy's boat. He then picks up a cushion, and starts a 'pillow fight' with Stan and Babe.

Ollie throws a cushion at Charlie, but he ducks and the cushion hits someone else (also in a boat) and they are knocked into the lake. His boat in turn hits another boat and two more people end up in the lake. The first

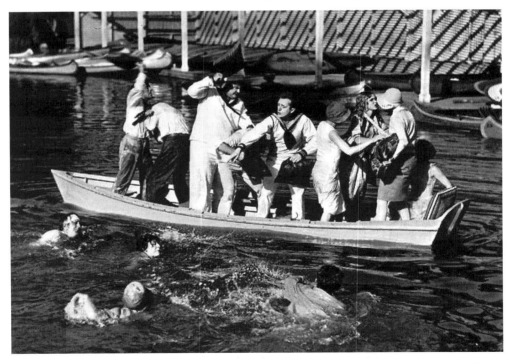

*Charlie (on the left in the boat) in the Laurel and Hardy film 'Men O' War'. This was Charlie's first talking part in a Laurel and Hardy film.*

guy (Baldwin Cooke) who was knocked into the water, climbs into the boat occupied by Charlie, Stan and Ollie and the two girls.

"Who threw that cushion?" he asks.

Stan points at Charlie and says, "He did."

"No I did not," Charlie replies.

A pillow fight starts with the new guy in the boat.

More and more people climb aboard the boat, until it eventually sinks, and this very funny film comes to an end.

So now we have heard Charlie's voice. There is no trace of a Birmingham accent, but his gruff tone would be perfect for the characters he would play.

Around this time, Charlie also appeared in the film 'Dad's Day' with Edgar Kennedy.

On the back of the photo (right) there is a hand written note by Charlie, which reads, "The fellow with his fists up is Hal Roach, showing Ed Kennedy and I a scene, from Dad's Day."

## They Go Boom

Charlie Hall would once again play the landlord in his next Laurel and Hardy film 'They Go Boom'.

Oliver Hardy has a cold, and as usual Stan is making the situation worse. They are making a lot of noise and it prompts Charlie to enter the room. He points at Ollie, "So it's you that's making all this noise. My tenants can't sleep. Why don't you be quiet like he is?" (he being Stan). Charlie leaves the room.

41

As we saw in the previous film, a mixture of pillows, Charlie, Laurel and Hardy do not go well together.

Ollie throws a pillow at Stan, which just happens to catch above the door. And who should walk again at this point? Yes, it's Charlie. Feathers from the pillow cascade down all over Charlie. And there are lots of them! This is followed by the pillow falling on Charlie's head.

Here we go again! Charlie kicks Ollie's backside. Ollie responds by pushing Charlie into the kitchen. The scene then cuts to the kitchen and we see Charlie with a tub over his head.

"I'll fix you," growls Charlie, and he storms out.

Laurel and Hardy go back to bed. They had begun pumping air into their mattress and it is still inflating. It inflates so much, that it almost touches the ceiling.

Charlie now re-enters with a policeman (Sam Lufkin). "This way officer," he says, and bumps straight into the over-inflated huge mattress. They fall backwards and Charlie pushes the policeman out of the way and leaves the

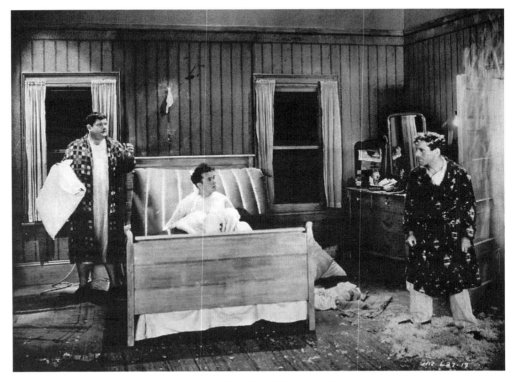

*Charlie confronts the boys again in the film 'They Go Boom'.*

room. Oliver Hardy then sneezes and the mattress explodes. Charlie enters the room again, this time with three police officers. "Officers arrest these two men," he says, and the film ends.

## The Hoose-Gow

For the second time in a Laurel and Hardy film, Charlie Hall had two parts. Yet he only has one line! The film is called 'The Hoose-Gow'. In this film Stan and Ollie are prison inmates sent to a labour camp to dig roads.

They are told to chop some wood. The more wood they chop, the more they will get to eat. Stan starts chopping a small piece of wood. Ollie reminds him that the more wood they chop, the more they will get to eat, and he points at a tree.

"Oh, the tree," says Stan.

And Oliver Hardy sets about chopping it down. The camera pans up the tree and you can hear someone snoring. It's the lookout, played by Charlie. The tree comes crashing to the ground with Charlie in it.

"Save me, oh God!" shouts Charlie, and his part in the film is finished.

Earlier on in the film Charlie can clearly be seen as one of the prison inmates getting out of the wagon.

## Blotto

There are plenty of arguments about which is Laurel and Hardy's best/funniest film. Everyone has his or her own favourite. My own particular favourite is 'Blotto' and once again Charlie makes an appearance, albeit right at the very end of the movie.

Stan and Ollie go to a club and get 'drunk' on Stan's wife's liquor – not knowing she has replaced it with cold tea (plus one or two other things as well!).

This film also contains my favourite clip from any Laurel and Hardy film. A cabaret singer (Frank Holliday) serenades the Boys with the song 'The Curse of an Aching Heart'. The words begin to make Stan feel sad and then cry. Ollie, himself close to tears, puts his arm around his friend to comfort him. It is a great scene from the two masters of comedy and you cannot help but be moved by watching it.

Just then, Stan's wife (Anita Garvin) enters the club, with a large shotgun wrapped in brown paper. By now the Boys think they are drunk and when Stan spots his wife he says to her, "We drank your liquor!"

"That wasn't liquor," she replies "that was cold tea."

Ollie smells the bottle and nods gently to the camera.

*Charlie as the cab driver in 'Blotto'.*

Both make a hasty exit from the club with Stan's wife in hot pursuit.

There is a cab waiting outside and the driver is Charlie Hall, in a large hat and a false moustache.

Ollie begs him to take them anywhere, and they drive off with Charlie sticking out his left arm. Stan's wife follows them into the street, raises the shotgun, and shoots at the cab.

And what a shot it is. The whole cab is blown apart. And although we see Stan and Ollie, incredibly Charlie doesn't appear to be in it.

A brilliant film, and I'm so pleased that the little man from Birmingham has a small part in it.

## Below Zero

The next few years would see Laurel and Hardy at their very best, and Charlie would remain with them.

In 'Below Zero', filmed in early 1930, Stan and Ollie are struggling street buskers, playing in heavy snow.

Despite the weather Oliver Hardy is singing 'In the Good Old Summer Time'. Just as he finishes his last note a snowball hits him in the face. He wipes it off his face in a way only Oliver Hardy could.

Charlie Hall has thrown the snowball.

"Ha! In the good old summer time," he growls.

Ollie is about to go over to him, but Stan stops him. "Ignore him. Just one of the lower elements," he says.

Charlie then begins to shovel the snow.

Laurel and Hardy continue to play 'In the Good Old Summer Time'. Annoyed at this, Charlie throws down his shovel and makes yet another snowball. But he decides not to throw it and he picks up his shovel and broom and walks off.

Just when you think this is the last you will see of him, another snowball hits Ollie in the face.

The camera cuts to Charlie, who is standing in a doorway. He nods, just to confirm it was he who threw it. It is the last we see of Charlie in this film.

As before, Charlie continued working with Charley Chase and Our Gang and once again appeared with Harry Langdon, this time in the film 'The Fighting Parson'.

'Below Zero' was filmed late February / early March in 1930. Shortly after this film was finished, Charlie heard the dreadful news that his father (Thomas) had passed away. His mother (Maria) was by his side when he died.

 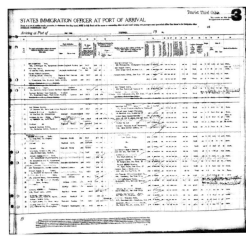

*Record of Maria's arrival in the US in 1930.*

A few months later and Maria Hall left Birmingham for the first time and arrived in New York on 3rd June 1930 to stay with her daughter Florence. What is interesting is that Maria gives the name of her nearest relative, as a friend Mrs. Jennie Reynolds, 144 Stuarts Road, Birmingham.

Charlie may have gone to visit his mother in New York, although he was about to start on his next Laurel and Hardy movie 'Pardon Us'.

## Pardon Us

Laurel and Hardy now ventured into feature films, the first of which was 'Pardon Us'. And as luck would have it, the little man from Birmingham had a part.

In this film Laurel and Hardy are convicts who get caught up in a prison break. Stan has a loose tooth that 'buzzes' every time he speaks, and so he is sent to the prison dentist.

Charlie plays the role of the dentist's assistant and is sitting at a desk. "Come on," says a warden (Wilfred Lucas) to Stan as they enter the room where Charlie is sitting.

The warden then turns to Charlie and says, "Here's another customer for ya. Fix him up."

"OK," says Charlie.

Charlie addresses Stan. "Hey rosebud, sit down."

Ollie enters the room and sits next to Stan. Stan is very pleased to see his friend and holds his arm for comfort.

"I sneaked in," says Ollie.

"Ollie" says Stan.

"What?"

"I'm scared."

"Why there's nothing to be afraid of. I'll stay right with you." Just then there is a lot of screaming and crashing from the dentist's room.

"Don't think about it," says Ollie.

The door opens, and Charlie wheels out a patient who is face-down in a very strange position.

"Alright rosebud," says Charlie to Stan. Stan points to the guy sitting next to him.

"Not him. You!"

Ollie leads Stan into the dentist's room.

"Come on sit down," says Charlie.

"Do you mind if I have my friend in here with me?" says Stan.

"OK."

A relieved Stan pushes the door open and it hits Ollie in the face.

"Ah, stop your playing," says Charlie, "Which one is it?"

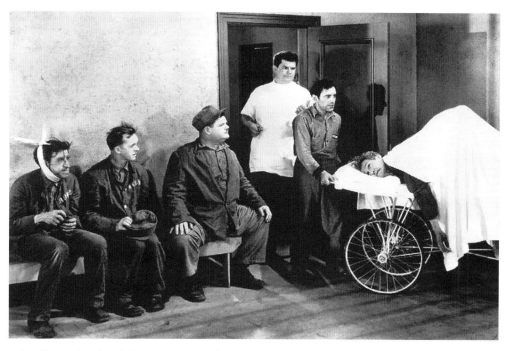

*Charlie as the dentist's assistant in 'Pardon Us'.*

"This one," says Stan.

Charlie flicks Stan's tooth

"Does it hurt?"

Stan shakes his head, "Uh-uh."

"Then what are you having it pulled for?"

"It's only loose. It buzzes," says Ollie.

"It buzzes?" says Charlie.

"Yes sir," says Stan and he makes a buzzing noise.

"OK, sit down."

Charlie goes over to the dentist (Otto Fries).

"Upper left molar doctor. It's a buzzer," he then leaves the room.

The dentist comes in and pulls a tooth from Ollie instead of Stan. But for Charlie his part is finished.

## Be Big

In 'Be Big', Stan and Ollie try to sneak out to a lodge meeting, without their wives knowing.

Ollie has come over 'sick' all of a sudden. He cannot make the weekend trip with his wife and Stan will have to stay to look after him.

A wonderfully sounding door bell chimes, and Charlie enters the room. He is dressed as a bellboy.

"Taxi's ready," he says.

He is asked to get the bags from the other room.

"Yes mam," he replies, and does so.

We don't see him again until the end of the film when he lets the wives back into the apartment.

*Chapter Seven*

# HIS FIRST LEADING ROLE

**Laughing Gravy**

Up until now, Charlie Hall's film appearances with Laurel and Hardy had been relatively small. But this was about to change. For in his next film with the pals Charlie was to play a starring role, and that film was 'Laughing Gravy'.

Stan and Ollie break the rules of a boarding house by keeping a dog in their room. The dog in question is called Laughing Gravy.

Oliver Hardy is begging Stan not to make so much noise, "Or the landlord will throw us out". He then gets into bed, which collapses. This makes some of the ceiling fall onto the head of the landlord who is sleeping in the room below. The landlord is of course Charlie Hall. The noise has set the dog barking.

Stan and Ollie hide Laughing Gravy in a bedside cabinet, just as Charlie enters the room.

"Where's that dog?" asks Charlie.

Ollie points out that it was Stan making the noise as he has the hiccups. To emphasise the point Stan hiccups. This causes the door to the bedside cabinet to open, to reveal Laughing Gravy.

"Aha!" says Charlie as he sees the dog and picks him up.

"You know my rules about dogs. I'm gonna throw him out."

"On a night like this?" says Ollie (there is heavy snow outside).

"Listen, if I wasn't so kind hearted, I'd throw you out too! Now get to bed." Charlie leaves the room with Laughing Gravy under his arm, and he throws him out onto the street.

"Go on get!" he snaps, and in his attempt to kick Laughing Gravy away, he slips over in the snow.

Of course Laurel and Hardy cannot leave their dog out in the cold and they decide to rescue it. Ollie goes outside and asks Stan to tie some sheets together so he can pass Laughing Gravy up to him. Apparently taking the dog through the front door might wake the landlord.

They manage to rescue the dog, but then Stan shuts the bedroom window leaving Ollie outside in the snow. An exasperated Ollie whistles to

Stan, but this awakens Charlie. He looks out of his window to see what is going on. Ollie hears the window open and hides behind a bush. He starts barking so the landlord will think it's Laughing Gravy.

"Get away from here, you little mutt," shouts Charlie, "Go on." He picks up a plant pot from his windowsill and throws it into the bush. It hits Ollie on the head, and he begins yelping like a dog.

Eventually Stan lets a frozen Ollie back into the room. After all their troubles it's time to get back into bed. But once again the bed collapses, and once again debris from the ceiling falls on Charlie waking him up.

Charlie storms up to the Boys' room and begins banging on the door. "Open this door!" he shouts, "Open this door."

This time Stan and Ollie hide Laughing Gravy up the chimney. Charlie is outside the door and his patience has run out. He takes a few paces back and charges the door. Unfortunately for him, Stan opens it just as Charlie charges towards it. Charlie goes straight through into the kitchen and there is an enormous crash. He ends up with a cupboard over him and he struggles to free himself.

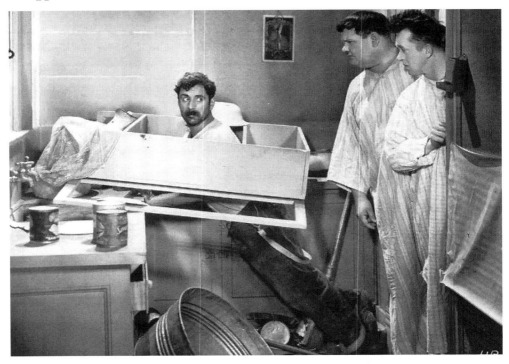

*This is more than he can stand. Charlie in the 1931 film 'Laughing Gravy'.*

Ollie opens the door to the kitchen and we see that Charlie has gone straight through the door, leaving a massive hole in it! "That settles it. Out you go, the first thing in the morning. Bag and baggage. You get me?" says Charlie.

By now Laughing Gravy has climbed up the chimney onto the roof and Laurel and Hardy decide to go up and get him down. Once again this wakes Charlie up and he quickly puts on his trousers. However, in his haste, he has comically put them on back to front.

Stan has managed to rescue Laughing Gravy and has gone back down the chimney. Oliver Hardy follows but demolishes the chimney stack going down.

Hearing the noise, Charlie opens his window again, just as a brick falls and hits him on the head, and a few seconds later another brick hits him. He is knocked out and collapses over the window ledge.

Back upstairs and the boys are washing Laughing Gravy in a tub in the middle of the room. There's a knock on the door, Ollie thinking it's Charlie, removes the dog and puts Stan's head in the tub and starts washing him. The door opens, to reveal a drunk (Charles Dorety) who has entered the wrong room!

Charlie starts to recover and awakes to find a huge lump on his head. The lump has become frozen with a tuft of hair on top of it. Charlie feels his sore head, and then slams the window shut. However he slams the window down with such force that the panes of glass fall out.

He's had enough and once again he storms upstairs and enters Stan and Ollie's room. Laurel and Hardy are still washing the dog, and this time seeing Charlie, Stan takes out the dog and pushes Ollie's head in the tub, and starts washing it!

Ollie then picks up the tub and throws it at Stan, it misses and Charlie takes a direct hit.

"Now you've gone and done it. If you're not out of here in 15 minutes, I'll send for the cops. So help me Bob!" shouts Charlie.

With an exaggerated swing of the arm, he leaves the room.

The first page of this book tells you how the film ends.

Charlie claimed that after this film was made, he went along with Stan and Ollie to the Fox Theatre in San Francisco. He has remembered the date wrongly, as they were actually there two years previously. However, Charlie gives us a good picture of what happened at the theatre when they made their personal appearance:

*"Talking of premieres reminds me of the opening of the Fox Theatre in San Francisco. Never has there been such a collection of stars in one place. William Fox outshone himself and hired a whole train to take the folks along. Was that train packed?*

*A couple of months later the manager pleaded with Hal Roach to let Laurel and Hardy make a personal appearance. The house was losing thousands of dollars and he said that the felt sure the boys would be able to push the receipts up a whole heap. Laurel and Hardy duly went, taking with them their excess luggage in the form of myself.*

*We also took a two-reel comedy entitled 'Laughing Gravy', which we had just finished.*

*Going along in the train I asked the boys what they intended to do for an act. "Oh!" says Babe casually, "just go on the stage and say 'Hullo' and perhaps introduce you as our menace, and tell the folks that you are the toughest guy in Hollywood, and so on. You know the sort of stuff Charlie."*

*We arrived at the theatre for the first house and were there crowds waiting to get in? The main feature was run through first, followed by 'Laughing Gravy' which in its turn was followed by Laurel and Hardy's personal appearance. It was fully a couple of minutes before the boys could open their mouths there was such pandemonium.*

*Then they put on a few gags and introduced me. I had done myself proud for the occasion and had on a new suit. Perhaps I looked a bit cocky in it, for Babe glared at me and said, "So you're the little tough guy who kicks me on the shins – eh? You're the chap who pokes me in the eye?"*

*"Yes," I answered proudly, "I am."*

*"And you're the one who kicks me out of bed in the middle of the night, are you?" "Sure I am," I said, beaming all over my face, and getting still more pleased with myself, I added, "What are you going to do about it, anyway?"*

*That crack cost me plenty. Stan gave Babe the well-known nod and grin and they started to cut the top of my hat, which I was holding. Babe tore my collar and the top off my shirt. They ripped my brand new suit off my back between them and chased me off the stage clad only in my vest and pants.*

*When we got back to the dressing room the boys just stood laughing, mighty pleased with themselves.*

*"What came over you guys?" I asked. "What made you do it?"*

*Babe explained that if I hadn't looked so darned cocky and self-satisfied nothing would have happened.*

*"Never mind Charlie," said Stan. "It won't happen again." That was all he knew.*

*The manager came along and asked if they would mind (they would mind, mark you) giving an extra performance a day and go through the same routine. Of course, from then on, we had to do this every day during our stay, and we broke all records for the house right through the run.*

*We made 32 appearances that week, which meant 32 suits, 32 hats, 32 collars and ties. Apart from the record in the theatre, I guess it was a boom time in the tailoring business as well."*

*Charlie hangs on to his bucket, in the 1931 film 'Air Tight'.*

There is in fact some truth in this story, although it was well rehearsed. Charlie would be sitting in the audience and he would be called out on stage. His suit would be a prop that rips easily.

Stan and Ollie would use this routine again with different actors.

On the subject of 'Laughing Gravy', in the Spanish version (Las Calaveras) and the French version (Les Carottiers) Charlie's voice was dubbed.

It was in this year that we believe Charlie made his first appearance with his pal Edgar Kennedy in Edgar's 'Average Man' series, although we cannot be sure.

Edgar Kennedy had just moved to RKO.

The film was 'Lemon Meringue' which was the first official entry of the 'Average Man' series.

Bill Cassara who wrote the excellent book 'Edgar Kennedy, Master of the Slow Burn' gives his opinion on this:

*Although the film (Lemon Meringue) is "missing", I recall going through the script held at an off storage near UC at LA. I would have written down Charlie Hall in the cast, but none of the extras were cast yet. There was once a part for the pie man delivery man, and described as, "A very good bit". That to me says Charlie all over it, but I cannot say I saw his name in that form.*

If Charlie did get the part of 'the pieman' in 'Lemon Meringue', he was paid $25, and the cast was provided with 75 cents for lunch. Bill tells us that over 1000 pies were used in the film. We can only hope one day this film will turn up.

Another film Charlie appeared in this year is 'Air Tight', directed by his good friend George Stevens. The film was made at the Hal Roach Studios as part of 'The Boy Friends' series. Although Charlie isn't listed in the film credits, he does have a fairly large part in the film.

But it's a very messy part for Charlie. He gets mowed down into a pool of mud, he has a bucket of paint thrown out of a glider land on his head, he ends up in a bucket of white wash, and finally has a bucket of black paint fall on his head. All in the line of comedy!

**Come Clean**
Next we move onto 'Come Clean', a wonderful film, which has a wonderful part for Charlie.

In this film Mr and Mrs Laurel pay a visit to Mr and Mrs Hardy.

Stan decides that he wants some ice cream, so the Boys set out to buy some. Stan Laurel and Oliver Hardy enter a store to buy the ice cream, which just happens to be run by Charlie Hall.

In one of their great encounters with Charlie, this scene is a favourite of all Laurel and Hardy fans worldwide. No one could menace the word "Chocolate" like Charlie Hall.

At first Charlie is pleased to see them, but as Stan aggravates him, his manner becomes more and more aggressive. Here is the build up to the famous chocolate rant.

"Good evening," says Charlie.

"Good evening sir," replies Ollie.

"What can I do for yers?"

"We would like a quart of your best ice cream please."

"Yes sir. What flavour?" Charlie replies.

"What flavours have you?"

"Strawberry, pineapple and vanilla."

Ollie turns to Stan and asks him "What flavour do you want?"

"I'll have chocolate," says Stan.

"I'm sorry but we're out of chocolate," says Charlie.

Stan continues, "Have you any mustachio?"

"No, we're out of mustachio."

"You're out of mustachio."

"Yes," says Charlie.

Stan then turns to Ollie "He's out of mustachio."

"Mm-hm," says Ollie.

Stan turns back to Charlie. "What other flavours are you out of?"

"Strawberry – We're out of orange, gooseberry and chocolate," snaps Charlie.

"Alright," says Stan, "I'll have it without chocolate."

An exasperated Ollie joins in. "Didn't the gentleman just tell you that he didn't have any chocolate."

Stan continues, "I just told the gentleman, that I didn't want….."

Ollie has heard enough. He turns to Charlie and says, "Just give us a quart of any kind that's handy, please."

"Yes, sir." Charlie places the ice cream on the counter.

But Stan has to get involved again.

"What flavour's that?" he asks.

"Chocolate!" shouts Charlie.

If you haven't seen this film, I highly recommend that you do.

## Beau Hunks

Charlie Hall, as we have seen, had some very small parts in films with Laurel and Hardy. But it is almost impossible to get a smaller part than his next appearance with them in 'Beau Hunks'.

Stan and Ollie join the Foreign Legion to forget the woman who broke Ollie's heart.

A line of new recruits shouts out their numbers. Charlie is number thirteen, and "Thirteen!" is all he says in this film.

He can however be spotted in the background making his bed, as Stan and Ollie realise that the woman who broke Ollie's heart (Jeannie Weenie, aka Jean Harlow) has done the same to a few other recruits.

## On the Loose

'On the Loose' is in fact a Thelma Todd and Zasu Pitts comedy made at the Hal Roach Studios.

Laurel and Hardy make a cameo appearance in this film, as a favour for Hal Roach. Charlie plays the part of a shooting gallery attendant at the Coney Island Fair.

Thelma Todd approaches the stall where Charlie is working.

"Well hello sister," he says.

Thelma has apparently been to the fair before, but doesn't want her date (John Loder) to know, so she shoots the hat off Charlie's head, to stop Charlie talking. Her date shoots and misses a couple of times, but thinks he has done well. "25 cents please," says Charlie.

Thelma's date then offers her a wager than she cannot better him. She then picks up a gun and fires four shots and knocks down four squirrels. With her left hand she picks up another gun and this time shoots and hits five squirrels.

"Beginners luck," she says.

Charlie places his elbow on the counter and puts his head in his hand. He then does an 'Oliver Hardy' and looks straight at the camera.

Charlie made quite a few appearances with Thelma Todd and Zasu Pitts during his time at Hal Roach. These would range from walk on parts, to a small amount of dialogue.

Today the Todd and Pitts, and the Charley Chase films are becoming more popular. Some of them are very funny and are certainly worth viewing.

**Any Old Port**

In this film Laurel and Hardy anger their landlord Mugsie (Walter Long) by helping Mugsie's reluctant fiancée to escape.

As you would expect in a Laurel and Hardy film, it just so happens that later Stan has to face Mugsie in a boxing match!

Charlie plays the part of Stan's 'boxing second' and is helping Stan prepare for his fight against Mugsie.

"Hang onto him kid," says Charlie "It's your only chance."

"How do you mean?" asks Stan.

"Hold him in the clinches and don't let go."

The fight scene with Stan and Walter Long is hilarious, and Charlie makes a brief appearance at the very end of the film. Incredibly Stan defeats Mugsie after picking up Mugsie's 'loaded' boxing glove!

**The Music Box**

In December 1931 Laurel and Hardy began work on what is possibly their most famous film, called 'The Music Box' (it was released in April 1932).

This is the film where Laurel and Hardy deliver a piano up a long flight of steps. If you talk to anyone about Laurel and Hardy, this film will always crop up in the conversation.

"What was the name of the film where they carry the piano up the steps?" is a very common question.

Well the answer is of course 'The Music Box'.

Laurel and Hardy are first seen driving a horse drawn cart with the piano on the back. Charlie plays the part of a postman, and Ollie stops him to ask for directions to the house where the piano is to be delivered.

"Pardon me, Mr Postman," says Ollie.

"Yes Sir," replies Charlie.

"Could you tell me where 1127 Walnut Avenue is?"

"1127 Walnut Avenue?"

This time Ollie replies, "Yes Sir."

"That's the house up there, right on top of the stoop."

In front of the stoop, is what appears to be a very long flight of steps.

After various attempts, the boys finally manage to get the piano to the top of the steps, and once again they encounter Charlie.

"Did you fellas carry that piano all the way up these stairs?" he asks.

Stan nods.

"You didn't have to do that. You see that road down there. All you have…"

Before Charlie can finish his sentence, the piano starts moving. He helps the boys to stop it, and then repeats his sentence.

"All you had to do was to drive around that road to the top here."

"Phew," sighs Charlie and off he goes.

Incredibly Laurel and Hardy take the piano back down the steps to deliver it by road!

In 1932 at the Ambassador Hotel's Coconut Grove, 'The Music Box' won a certificate as the Academy of Motion Picture Arts and Sciences' choice for 'Best Short Subject' (Comedy).

Today the film is as funny as when it was made, and you can visit the steps in Los Angles. They are situated on Vendome Street, and there is even a sign that reads 'Music Box Steps'.

It was around this time that Hal Roach was planning a new series of films teaming up Charlie Hall with Charley Rogers as airline pilots. However, the series never materialised, and it is not known why. There was talk of Charley Rogers being injured when suspended from a plane, and some footage was used in the film 'Wild Babies' in which Charlie had a small part as an explorer's man.

*Charlie with his wife Wilda (left) and his mother Maria.*

Charlie also had a part in the film 'Million Dollar Legs', which included W.C. Fields, and he continued working with Charley Chase.

The year is now 1932 and it was in this year that Charlie met a dancer by the name of Wilda George. The meeting took place at a party given by Charley Chase.

Wilda George was born in Malvern, Iowa, USA on July 27th 1899.

She formed an act with her sister (Florence) called 'The George Sisters' (Toots and Foxie) and Wilda used the name 'Foxie'.

Charlie and Wilda soon became an item, and Wilda even appeared as an extra in one of the Laurel and Hardy films called 'Our Relations'.

### Pack up your Troubles

Laurel and Hardy's next film was a feature, called 'Pack up your Troubles'. Stan and Ollie are left looking after their friend's little girl (played by Jacquie Lyn) after he is killed in the First World War.

Stan and Ollie are trying to hide their friend's baby from the authorities, who want to place her in care.

They realise they have been tracked down and they need to hide the child. They put her into a dumb waiter and send it down.

Charlie plays the part of a janitor, and is there when the dumb waiter appears.

"Hey come out of there," he says to Jacquie. "That's no place for you to play in. Go and sit over there till I get through."

This is all we see of him in the film.

**Twice Two**

In 'Twice Two' Laurel and Hardy play each others' wives at a fraught anniversary dinner.

After a disastrous evening, Ollie and his wife are about to leave. Just before they do, there's a knock on the door.

It's Charlie with a large cake.

"Does Mrs. Laurel live here?" he asks.

"Yes," says Ollie's wife (played by Stan).

"Here's the cake she ordered this morning. Will you see that she gets it?"

"I certainly will."

Mrs. Hardy (Stan) pulls the cover off the cake, and Charlie touches his cap and leaves.

No guesses how Mrs. Hardy lets Mrs. Laurel have the cake!

In 1933 Charlie appeared in various Hal Roach comedies with Thelma Todd, Zasu Pitts, Charley Chase, Edgar Kennedy and Patsy Kelly to name a few. And as we have seen, Charlie always seemed to manage to get a part in Laurel and Hardy's most famous films.

Charlie is also credited with being in another famous film, and that is the original 'King Kong,' which starred Fay Wray. The film was made by RKO and Charlie knew Fay from her time at the Hal Roach Studios. It is claimed that Charlie was an extra (ship's crew member) in 'King Kong', but this it difficult to prove one way or the other. His part in the film may have been cut, or it is just too difficult to spot him.

**Me and My Pal**

'Me and My Pal', is Charlie's next appearance with Laurel and Hardy. In this film a jigsaw stops everyone from getting to Ollie's wedding. James Finlayson is waiting for Oliver Hardy to show up to marry his daughter. But Ollie has been delayed due to the fact that Stan has bought him a jigsaw puzzle as a wedding present. Stan starts piecing the jigsaw together, and it seems everyone from the cab driver to a policeman cannot resist trying to do it. In the meantime, Charlie delivers a large wreath to the wedding party with 'In memory' on the front.

"What's the wreath for?" asks Fin.

"I don't know. Mr Laurel picked it out himself and told me to bring it over here," says Charlie.

"Haven't you any bit of sense than bring a wreath to a wedding?"

"It's nothing to do with me. Orders is orders."

Fin calls for his car, and then takes the wreath off Charlie.

"I may have use for this!"

Charlie nods.

## Midnight Patrol

Next on the list for Charlie comes 'Midnight Patrol', which sees Laurel and Hardy as hapless police officers. Stan and Ollie are eating their supper in a police car when they receive a call on their radio. The scene then cuts to the back of their car where Charlie and another villain (Robert Kortman) are trying to steal their spare tyre!

"Calling car 13," comes from the radio.

"That's us," says Ollie.

"Calling car one-three."

"I thought he said 13," says Stan.

"Shut up!" Ollie replies.

The voice continues on the radio.

"Look out boys, someone is stealing your spare tyre. That is all."

Ollie turns to Stan. "See who that is," and he pushes Stan. "Go ahead."

Stan gets out of the car to see who's stealing their spare tyre.

"Look out Hank," says Charlie, and they drop their tools and run to their own car.

Stan confronts them. "If you come back here again, I'll arrest you."

Hank replies, "Who will?"

"I..... We will," says Stan.

With his hand on his hip and a stamp of his foot, Charlie replies in a very comical manner, "Oh is that so?"

"Ye-" says Stan (he doesn't finish the word yes) mimicking Charlie with his hand on his hip.

He then picks up a brick and throws it at the two villains. It misses them but goes straight through the back window of their car!

Realising what he has done, Stan quickly returns to his police car and gets in. He is sitting next to Ollie, when a brick is thrown through the police car back window and hits Ollie on the back of the head, causing his milk to shoot out all over his face. We can only presume that Charlie threw the brick.

## Busy Bodies

Still in 1933, Charlie meets up with Laurel and Hardy again in the film 'Busy Bodies', set in a sawmill.

Stan and Ollie arrive for work in their trusty Model T Ford. They pull behind Charlie who is gathering some wood. Ollie beeps the horn, which sends Charlie into an exaggerated panic, and he drops all the wood.

Ollie laughs.

"What do you think you are trying to do?" asks Charlie in a frightened state.

"Can't you take a little joke?" says Ollie, and wiggles his tie.

"Why don't you look where you're going?" says Charlie, and his first part in this movie is finished.

Later on, Oliver Hardy (with Stan's help) has managed to get his hands stuck in a window frame he is making.

Stan stands on the frame to pull him out, and in doing so they both fall on Charlie who is walking past.

They all get to their feet.

"That's the second time you've picked on me," says Charlie. And he punches Ollie in the face.

Stan then punches Charlie under the chin (which causes Charlie's cap to come off). Charlie does the same to Stan, and they both pick their hats up. Stan then holds out his right arm, but hits Charlie with an upper cut from his left arm. Charlie's cap again comes off. Charlie now tries to punch Stan, but Stan is too quick and he removes his hat. Stan puts his hat back on. Charlie now hits Stan in the face again, and again Stan's hat falls off. Stan responds, and tries to slap Charlie, but Charlie ducks and Stan hits Ollie in the face instead.

"Ha Ha," laughs Charlie, and he slaps Stan on the back.

"Thanks buddy. You know I kinda like you."

"You do?" says Stan.

"You bet I do. You got a kind face."

"Thanks," says Stan.

Ollie cannot believe what he is seeing and looks into the camera.

"Have a cigar," Stan says to Charlie.

"Don't mind if I do."

Once again this causes Ollie to look at the camera.

"Sit down," says Stan.

"Thanks," says Charlie.

Stan lights Charlie's cigar, and Charlie starts to puff away.

Stan now whistles to the foreman (Tiny Sandford) who comes over to see what he wants.

Stan points to the 'No Smoking' sign on the wall, and then points to Charlie who is smoking. The foreman picks Charlie up by the scruff of the neck, and carries him out.

Charlie cries, "You dirty double crossers. I'll see you guys at lunchtime. Double cross a pal?"

We hear a big crash as Charlie is thrown out.

Later on in the film Oliver Hardy is stuck in some ducting high above the ground. Stan then climbs a ladder, and proceeds to help him out. Of course it ends up with both of them crashing to the ground. As the Boys come crashing down, we see Charlie and the foreman taking evasive action. Unfortunately Charlie falls straight into a large tub of whitewash.

He gets out and we see him covered from head to toe in paint.

## Sons of the Desert

We now move on to the film, which the Laurel and Hardy Appreciation Society is named after, the wonderful 'Sons of the Desert'.

Oliver Hardy feigns an illness, so that he and Stan can attend a convention. A convention which their wives were set against!

Charlie only has a walk on part in this film.

Laurel and Hardy are at the convention having a great time, and are sitting at the same table as Charley Chase. As Stan and Ollie call for champagne, Charlie Hall appears as the second waiter who brings the glasses.

## Oliver the Eighth

In this film, Stan sells their barber's shop after Ollie answers an ad from a millionairess (Mae Busch) looking for a husband.

Unfortunately, Charlie Hall's part in 'Oliver the Eighth' was cut. Originally, he was cast as the laundryman, who collects the dirty towels off Stan. Charlie only had a few lines in the film, and maybe one-day, his part of the film will be found. However, I found another version of this story line in the 'Boys Cinema Annual' of 1935. It reads as follows:

### The Unposted Letter

*And what of Stanley?*

*Poor deserted Stanley, left all alone in the shop, with all its unpaid bills. At first he was numb, feeling nothing, understanding nothing, but slowly the full horror of his position trickled into his brain. He was alone!*

*It was too much! Putting his head in his hands, Stan burst into tears and sobbed as if his heart would break.*

*"Good morning," said a voice almost in his ear. "What's the matter?"*

*Stan jumped as if he had been shot. Standing before him was a seedy-looking person with eyes so close together that for one awful moment Stan thought that the stranger had only one eye set in the middle of his forehead.*

*The look of the stranger was certainly not one to inspire confidence, but Stanley was always a trusting soul, and soon he was telling his new friend all his troubles.*

*"And Ollie's left me with the shop," he concluded, "and I don't know how to sell it."*

*"That's easy," said his new-found friend. "I'll buy it."*

*"What will you give me for it?" asked Stan.*

*"This," said the stranger, and fumbling in his overcoat pocket he brought out something the size and shape of an ordinary brick, but yellow in colour, with the words SOLID GOLD in big black letters on it.*

*"I haven't any money, but I'll exchange this gold brick for your shop, and it's a bargain." (But he didn't say who was getting the bargain.)*

*Stanley hesitated.*

*"And I'll tell you what I'll do," said the man. "I'll throw these in too."*

*And digging down in his pocket again he fished out a handful of peanuts and held them to Laurel.*

*That clinched the deal!*

*"Done!" said Stanley. "Just wait till I put this apron away, and the shop's yours."*

*Chapter Eight*

# CHARLIE STARS IN DOUBLE BILL

**Them Thar Hills**

Charlie's small part in 'Sons of the Desert' was in stark contrast to his major role in Laurel and Hardy's next film 'Them Thar Hills', made in 1934. In fact Charlie was to take the lead role for the first time since 'Laughing Gravy'.

Stan and Ollie take a trip to the mountains, as this is prescribed to cure Ollie's gout. Charlie and his wife (Mae Busch) have run out of gas and are walking along the road. Charlie cuts quite a figure in white plus fours, white shoes and a white cap.

"Oh I told you when we passed the last station to get some gas. But would you pay any attention to me?" says Mae.

"Awe shut up," Charlie snarls back.

"I won't shut up."

We move onto Laurel and Hardy who are getting very drunk in a trailer. Unbeknown to them they are drinking water from a well, in which bootleg liquor has been poured.

"Oh look," says Mae, "There's some people over there with a trailer. Maybe we could get some gas from them?"

"Maybe," says Charlie.

"Oh," says Mae.

There is a knock on the trailer door.

"Come in," says Ollie.

Charlie has a wonderful line in which he introduces his wife.

"Sorry to trouble ya. My name's Mr. Hall, this is the missus."

"What can I do for you?" Ollie replies.

"We're out of gas. If you have some to spare, I'd like to buy it."

"Why certainly, there's a spare can on the floor, just help yourself."

"Thanks a lot."

Seeing the boys drinking Mae says, "Could I have a drink of water. I'm so thirsty."

"Why certainly," says Ollie.

"Do you want some?" Mae says to Charlie, (after tasting it).

"No," he snaps back.

"OK baby, you don't know what you're missing."

"Hey come on," says Charlie.

"Oh you get the car and bring it here. I'm all in."

She turns to the Boys. "You don't mind if I wait here?"

"Why certainly not," replies Ollie.

"Thanks," says Charlie.

"You're welcome."

"Thanks," says Mae, "Say, this is delicious," as she tastes the water again.

"That's the iron in it," says Ollie.

Charlie leaves, but returns soon after to hear Stan, Ollie and Mae all singing and acting very drunk. Mae has a Bowler Hat on her head, and Ollie is playing a guitar. Charlie is not impressed as he looks on through the trailer window.

He goes in.

"Hey, what's going on here?"

"Oh baby," says Mae.

"Don't 'oh baby' me. What are you drinking?"

"Good Ole Mountain water."

Charlie tastes it and spits it out. He shouts at Mae.

"You get out of here."

"I don't wanna," she replies.

"I said get out of here."

At this point Ollie interrupts. "Don't talk to that lady like that."

Charlie shouts back at him, "You shut up. Get out of here. Come on," and he knocks the bowler off Mae's head. "I said get out of here and get in that car."

"Bye fellas," says Mae.

"Bye," is the reply from Stan and Ollie.

"Pom, pom, come again," says Stan.

Charlie is now very angry and he asks, "What do you mean getting my wife drunk?" and he punches Ollie in the face.

Stan then picks up a plate of butter, takes off Charlie's hat and pushes the butter onto the top of Charlie's head.

This gets a loud laugh from Ollie, which is brought to an abrupt end when Charlie hits him in the face again.

He now turns his attention to Stan, and he pushes Stan's head into the bucket of mountain water on the table. He holds it there until Ollie slaps his hand.

Charlie's response is to hit Ollie again.

It's now Stan's turn and he sharpens a knife, and with it he cuts a piece of hair off Charlie's head. He then takes a spoon, dips it into a can of molasses and rubs it over Charlie's chin. The piece of hair is then stuck onto Charlie's chin, and it looks like he has a 'goatee' beard.

Charlie looks at the camera.

Ollie again laughs out loud, and again Charlie hits him.

Stan now takes a plunger, dips it into the bucket and sticks it onto Charlie's head.

Ollie can be heard laughing out loud again. Charlie tries to pull the plunger off his head, but it is stuck fast, and he comically pulls at it.

Ollie is still finding this very funny, so Charlie points to the ceiling. When Ollie looks up, Charlie flicks him in the throat (there is a wonderful sound effect to match this).

Stan now reaches down and picks up a set of bellows. He dips them into a coffee pot, sucks up some coffee and points it at Charlie. However Charlie takes the bellows off Stan and points them back at him. Stan puts his finger over the end of the bellows just as Charlie squeezes it and the coffee squirts back all over his face.

Surprise, surprise, Ollie laughs again.

Charlie turns around to wipe his face, and he is now standing with his back to the boys, who are still sitting at the table.

Stan now cuts Charlie's belt at the back and his trousers fall down. Ollie is laughing so much that he bangs the table and a plate of beans (that just happens to be on the edge of the table) fall into Charlie's trousers (if you look closely you can see the plate of beans jump off the table before Ollie hits it).

Ollie takes the plate back, and shows us that it is now empty of beans.

Charlie pulls up his trousers, notices the beans and says, "I'll fix you for this," and walks out.

The Boys are still very drunk and begin singing, "La la la la la la la la la la! Pom Pom!"

Charlie is now outside, and he unhitches the trailer from the car. It tips over, causing Stan, Ollie and all the contents to spill out.

The Boys pick themselves up and survey the damage. Charlie comes over and nods, as if to say "I did that".

Still the battle isn't over.

Oliver Hardy picks up the can of molasses and pours it very slowly all over Charlie. Stan then passes a pillow to his friend who throws the feathers from the pillow over Charlie.

Charlie is in a right mess, tarred and feathered. He is still holding up his trousers and he looks directly into the camera and blows some feathers from his mouth.

Laurel and Hardy turn their back on Charlie, who hasn't finished yet. He picks up an oil can and pours the contents over Ollie's behind.

"You gotta match?" he says to Stan.

Stan hands one over and Charlie lights it, and sets fire to Ollie's behind. Now he has finished and he walks off.

Ollie is panicking, as a lot of smoke is bellowing from his posterior.

"Why don't you jump in the well. The water will put it out," says Stan.

We just see Charlie's car drive off as Ollie shakes Stan's hand, "Thank you," he replies.

He dives into the well and there is an enormous explosion.

Ollie is blasted in to the air like a rocket, and Stan watches as he finally comes down and crashes into the ground headfirst.

It's the end of another very funny film, as we see Ollie's legs kicking into the air.

Charlie was to star in a sequel to this film, but before this, he appeared in another Laurel and Hardy short 'The Live Ghost'.

## The Live Ghost

Laurel and Hardy help to press-gang the crew of a ship, and end up on the boat themselves.

The film starts with a crowd of men inside a bar. Charlie can be seen in a striped T-shirt, taking a cigarette from behind his ear and putting it in his mouth.

Walter Long (the ship's Captain) is looking for a crew, but no one will sail with him, as they think his ship is haunted. He asks the help of Stan and Ollie to get him a crew, and offers them a dollar for every person they get.

They have a simple plan. Stan will go in to the bar and Ollie will stay outside with a 'clunker' (a frying pan).

Stan goes into the bar clutching a bag of eggs, and heads for Charlie's table. Charlie is in conversation with a guy (Leo Willis) at his table.

"Did you ever see that guy again?" he says to Charlie.

"No, I haven't seen him for months," Charlie replies.

Their conversation is broken up by Stan (who sits at their table) and he takes an egg out of the bag.

"What are you gonna do with that egg?" asks Charlie's pal.

"I bet you a dollar, you can't put it in your mouth without breaking it" says Stan.

Charlie responds to his friend, "Ha, go on take him on. Remember what you did to that billiard ball?"

"That's a sinch. Get your buck ready."

He puts the egg into his mouth, and Stan hits him under the chin.

Charlie starts to laugh.

The guy gets up and chases Stan out of the bar. Ollie is waiting and hits the guy on the head with the frying pan. He is knocked out, and Walter Long gives Ollie a dollar and carries the guy off. He takes him to the ship and drops him down into the hold.

This happens several times, and the bodies of the men are piling up on top of each other.

Ollie now has an idea and he says to Stan, "I'd better go in this time. They know you by now." They swap the bag of eggs and frying pan with each other and Ollie tells Stan to "Lay it on heavy."

Ollie walks into the bar, clutching the bag of eggs, and he sees Charlie who acknowledges him. He sits at Charlie's table and takes out an egg.

*In the same year (1934) Charlie appeared in 'Kentucky Kernels' with Wheeler and Woolsey.*

"What are you gonna do with that?" asks Charlie.

"I'll bet you a dollar, that you can't put this egg in your mouth without breaking it," replies Ollie.

"Can you do it?" says Charlie.

"Why of course."

"You do it first, then I'll do it."

They shake hands. Ollie puts the egg into his mouth, and Charlie hits him under the chin and starts laughing. Ollie looks at the camera, as he has swallowed the egg. This has made Charlie laugh even harder and he does so with his mouth open. Ollie takes another egg out of the bag and puts it into Charlie's mouth. He then hits Charlie on top of his head and under his chin simultaneously. The egg breaks in Charlie's mouth.

"Why you…" He stops his sentence and chases Ollie out of the bar.

"You maniac," he shouts at Ollie, as he chases him around a lamp-post.

Stan is trying to hit Charlie on the head with the frying pan, but he keeps missing. Eventually he hits Ollie, and then, finally, he hits Charlie. They both collapse on the floor.

Walter Long appears, and is pleased to see two more for his 'ghost ship' but Stan hits him on the head as well. Walter takes the frying pan off Stan and hits him with it.

The scene cuts to the ship, where bodies of the men are piled up on top of each other and there are plenty of groaning noises.

They realise that they have being shanghaied, and close in threateningly on Stan and Ollie. However Walter Long saves them, and offers them protection as long as they are aboard his ship.

Later the ship has apparently docked in 10 ports, but Laurel and Hardy refuse to disembark.

"Going ashore?" they are asked.

"Uh uh" says Ollie, knowing they are safe on board.

While ashore a number of the crew think it would be a good idea go back to the ship to "Fix those two guys who Shanghaied us."

"Swell. I want the big guy," says Charlie.

The crew re-board the ship, only to see Arthur Housman wandering about covered head to toe in whitewash. They think he's a ghost, and all jump overboard.

**Tit For Tat**

This is the sequel to 'Them Thar Hills'. So once again, Charlie gets to play the leading role.

Laurel and Hardy have opened up an "electrical supplies" shop, and Ollie suggests they go and meet their neighbours.

"I'm going over to Mr. Hall's to pay my respects to our neighbour," says Ollie.

"That's a good idea," says Stan. "I'd like to meet him too."

"Come along."

They go next door to meet Mr. Hall.

"Er, good morning Mr. Hall. I'm Mr. Hardy and this is my partner Mr. Laurel."

Charlie sounds unimpressed. "Is that so?"

Ollie carries on, "Er, we're opening an electrical store next door."

"So what?" replies Charlie who already sounds annoyed.

He then stares at them, as if he recognises them.

Ollie asks Stan,

"What's he looking at?"

Stan replies, "Remember that fella who we met in the trailer? Remember his wife came in and she asked for a drink of water?"

Just then Mrs. Hall (Mae Busch) starts singing, "Tra la la la la la la la la la la."

"Pom pom." Stan finishes it off.

Both men turn around and see Mrs. Hall.

Ollie claps his hands and says, "I remember you."

To which Charlie replies, "And I remember you too. Now get out of my store and stay out."

"Aw, don't be like that. Let bygones be bygones. You have a business and we have a business. Let's help each other. You send people over to our store, and we'll send people to your store. What do you say?"

Ollie holds out his hand for Charlie to shake, but Charlie is having none of it. "You mind your business and I'll mind my business. Now get out of here before I throw you out."

"Be it as it may. Remember beggars can't be choosers. You go your way and we'll go our way."

"You're right Ollie," says Stan.

"We'll take the high road and let him take the low road."

"Henceforth we'll neither nod nor speak. Come Stanley."

Stan and Ollie exit Charlie's store.

Charlie turns to Mae. "Didya hear me tell 'em baby?"

"You sure did Daddy," Mae replies.

"When I tell em, they stay told. No beating around the bush with me."

"That's right."

Meanwhile, Ollie is on a ladder outside, putting in some more light bulbs. The ladder just happens to be on a lift, which Stan presses. Ollie goes up on the ladder and ends up on next door's upper window.

Mae, who has gone upstairs, opens the window and sees Ollie.

"Wha…" She cannot finish her word.

"Oh erm," says an embarrassed Ollie.

"I'm in a slight predicament. Would it be asking too much if I used your stairway."

"Oh my, it would be a pleasure. Come on in."

"Thank you."

Charlie is downstairs and he hears his wife laughing. He turns around to see Mae and Ollie coming down the stairs.

"I've never been in a position like that before," Ollie says. "But, it's certainly a pleasure to have seen you again."

Ever the gentleman, he tips his hat.

"Oh it's my pleasure," says Mae.

"Thank you so much. Goodbye."

"Goodbye."

*The Little Menace burns Ollie's nose in 'Tit For Tat'.*

At this point Ollie leaves. Charlie is not impressed and looks at the stairs where they have both come down.

It's now Charlie's turn to visit his new neighbours.

"Hey, just a minute you," he says to Ollie who is just coming back down the ladder. "What is the secret between you and my wife?"

"I have nothing to say," Ollie replies.

"Neither have I," says Stan.

"Listen weasel, you keep out of this," and Charlie pushes Stan into a bowl of light bulbs. He turns his attention again to Ollie.

"If I ever catch you even looking at my wife again, I'll hit you so hard, that he'll feel it."

"Is that so?"

"Yeah, that's so. And don't forget, the bigger they are, the harder they fall." Charlie nods his disapproval and leaves.

This has hurt Ollie, and he typically comes up with a wonderful response. "My character. It has been smirched. Ruthlessly dragged through the mud and mire."

"How do you mean?" asks Stan.

"Didn't you hear him accuse me of having a clandestine meeting with his wife? Never let it be said that a Hardy's spotless reputation should be so maliciously trodden upon. Come Stanley."

"Where are you going?"

"I'm going to demand an apology."

Stan comes back with a classic retort. "You're right Ollie. He who filters your good name steels trash!"

"Come Stanley."

Back in Hall's Groceries, Charlie is having a go at Mae. "The next time you tell me to keep an eye on the store, I'm gonna keep the other eye on you."

"Oh you make me sick," Mae replies.

Laurel and Hardy march in unison back into Charlie's store and approach him.

"Whadda you want?" snaps Charlie.

"Pardon the intrusion," says Ollie.

"But I have come to seek redress for the gross insult to my character. In other words I demand an apology."

Charlie gives him his answer. He hits him on the head with a wooden spoon.

Ollie now moves to the side of the counter and says, "I shall take this up with my barrister."

At this point he presses the till, and the drawer shoots out and hits Charlie on the chin, knocking his head backwards.

"Come Stanley."

On their way out, Stan picks up a marshmallow, but Ollie takes it off him and he puts it in his own mouth to Charlie's annoyance. Stan picks up another marshmallow and is about to put it into his mouth, but replaces it when he sees Charlie moving towards him. Charlie now follows the Boys back to their shop and this time Ollie is behind the counter.

"You've being picking on me all morning," says Charlie, holding a set of curling tongs in his hand. "Making my life miserable. If it's a fight you want. I'm the guy that'll give it you."

He hasn't noticed Stan has plugged in the tongs making him burn his hand. "Arrh," shouts Charlie and he drops them.

Ollie starts laughing, so Charlie places the tongs on to his nose, burning both sides. He then leaves the store, but the boys follow him.

Oliver Hardy scoops up a spoonful of cream cheese and flicks it into Charlie's face.

"Tit for Tat," he says to Stan.

"What?" replies Stan.

"Tit for Tat."

Stan takes his hat off.

"What's that for?"

"I thought you said tip me hat!"

"Come on."

They both pick up a marshmallow on the way out, and pointedly show it to Charlie before putting them into their mouths. Charlie goes over to the box of marshmallows, gets out a tin of 'Alum' powder and covers them with it. Yet again, Charlie goes next door. On the counter is a display of watches marked 'Special today $1.00'. Charlie takes all the watches off the display, puts them into a blender and plugs it in, as Laurel and Hardy look on. Eventually Stan stops the blender and Ollie takes the container out and peers inside it. All the watches have been blended into small parts. Ollie tips them out onto the counter. At this point Stan goes through the parts and picks out a piece and starts to spin it. He is pleased with his new toy and puts it into his pocket.

Back go the Boys to Hall's Groceries. Stan hands Ollie a jar of honey. He opens Charlie's till and pours the honey all over the contents. Charlie just stands and watches. He retaliates by taking Ollie's bowler hat and cutting off the top of it, in a meat slicer. Ollie looks through the hat into the camera. Stan now whispers to Ollie, who nods, and they walk over to another part of the shop. Charlie follows them and stands in between them. Stan and Ollie pick up a huge tub of 'Rex pure lard' and push it down onto Charlie's head. They remove the tub and Charlie is left with the lard stuck on his head (in the shape of the can). He starts to remove the lard from his face and he throws it to the floor.

"Come Stanley," says Ollie.

On the way out they once again pick up a marshmallow and put it into their mouths. To show their defiance, they put a second marshmallow into their mouths!

Back in their own shop and the 'Alum' powder begins to kick in. Their mouths become sucked in and they have difficulty speaking. Ollie fixes it by spraying their mouths with soda water.

Charlie now storms into their shop and goes berserk. He knocks and throws everything off the counter in a mad rage. He then gets a chair, stands on it and swings the row of ceiling lights into each other. They smash as they hit each other and the last one crashes through the shop window into the street. This causes a large crowd to gather.

"Now will you stop," shouts Charlie and gives a big nod of the head, before leaving.

Mae is looking out of the window and sees Charlie coming back.

Ollie takes off his coat and hands it to Stan. Back they go to Charlie's shop. This time the crowd follows them.

"I'm going to give you one more chance to apolo…" He doesn't finish his sentence as Charlie has scooped some cream cheese on a spoon and flicked it into Ollie's face. The same thing happens to Stan. The boys now walk over to a crate of eggs. Mae, hearing all the commotion, comes down the stairs.

"Hey, what's going on here?" she asks.

"You keep out of this," replies Charlie.

Stan and Ollie then sit Charlie into a crate of eggs. The crowd outside begins to laugh. Now Stan and Ollie pick up a second crate of eggs and tip them over Charlie's head. Charlie picks himself up just as a policeman (James C. Morton) enters the store.

"Now just a minute. Don't you think this has gone far enough? Who started this?" he asks.

Ollie points to Charlie, "He did."

"I did not," says Charlie.

"Why he did too. Why this little upstart in the presence of my friend, slandered my character for which I demanded an apology. He refused to give it. Hence this petty little argument."

"Slandered your character?" repeats the policeman.

"Yes sir. He filtered his good name. Didn't he?" says Stan.

"Filtered his good name," says the policeman.

"Why do you know what he did?" says Ollie.

"He accused me of a clandestine meeting with his wife (Mae gasps at this point) for which I was wholly and absolutely innocent."

"Then what were you doing coming downstairs with my wife?" says Charlie.

"Oh what nonsense. There was nothing to it," says Mae.

"Nothing to it officer," says Stan. "He was waiting for a streetcar!"

The policeman turns to Charlie, "Well it looks like you're to blame. You better apologise to this gentleman."

"I will not," snaps Charlie.

"Oh yes you will, or I will run you in."

"Well alright, but don't let it happen again."

Charlie holds out his hand for Ollie to shake.

*Stan and Ollie point the finger of blame at Charlie in 'Tit For Tat'.*

Ollie accepts his offer of a handshake and says, "No hard feelings."

Ollie, as chivalrous as ever, addresses Mae. "Madam," he says taking off his hat, "Allow me."

He takes her hand, kisses it, and says "goodbye".

Stan also decides to kiss Mae's hand, but Charlie kicks him up the backside, knocking his hat off!

The policeman hands it back to him and says, "Here come on, get out of here."

He then turns to Charlie, "You go back to your work. Go on."

And so the battle is over.

However, back at their own shop, Stan and Ollie are taken aback to see their entire stock has been loaded onto a truck by a man (Bobby Dunn) who has routinely been taking items from the shop each time they've been next door.

The film ends with the policeman putting a marshmallow into his mouth. As he tries to clear the crowd, he struggles to speak, due to the Alum powder on them.

This movie was to be Charlie's last major role in a Laurel and Hardy film.

# Chapter Nine

# LAST OF THE SHORTS
# AND MARRIAGE

## Thicker Than Water

1935, and in this film Oliver Hardy's savings get spent at an auction. After an argument with his wife about money, Ollie is feeling a little sorry for himself, so Stan has a bright idea. Incredibly Ollie listens to it.

Why doesn't he draw all his savings ($300) out of the bank and pay off the money he owes on his furniture?

After withdrawing the money from the bank, the Boys get drawn into an auction. They get sucked into bidding on behalf of a young lady (Gladys Gale) and end up buying a grandfather clock for $290, only for it to be run over by a truck on the way home.

In the meantime, Mrs. Hardy (Daphne Pollard) goes to the bank, where a very cheerful Charlie Hall is the bank teller.

"Good morning," she says.

"Good morning, Mrs. Hardy," Charlie replies.

"I wonder if you would do me a favour? You know I have a joint account with my husband, and I'd like you to fix it so that nobody else can draw the money out but me."

"I'd be glad to do it for you Mrs. Hardy, but your husband was here a short while ago."

"That's very nice, thank you – What! Did he take the money?"

"Yes ma'am, all of it. He closed the account."

At this point, Charlie Hall closed his account on making 'shorts' with Laurel and Hardy. In fact Charlie would only appear in a handful of films with his friends Stan Laurel and Oliver Hardy again. By the mid-30s, Laurel and Hardy switched to making feature films. Sadly, Charlie would only appear fleetingly in a few of them.

## Bonnie Scotland

His next appearance with Laurel and Hardy was in the feature film 'Bonnie Scotland'.

Charlie plays the part of a native henchman, but spotting him in this film is very difficult. Charlie wore a turban and had a false beard and moustache. During the film, Charlie brings on a cushion with two guns on it.

"What are these for?" says Ollie.

"You are to use those to blow you brains out" comes the reply.

At this point Stan starts to cry, "Ooh, I've never blow my brains out before."

*Charlie (right of screen) brings the guns.*

Yet another famous film Charlie is associated with is 'Top Hat', which starred Fred Astaire and Ginger Rogers. Again he is listed as an extra, but no trace of him can be found in the film.

At the end of the year Charlie Hall and Wilda George decided to get married, and they did so on 8th November 1935 in Yuma, Arizona, USA. Charlie invited all his brothers and his sister to his wedding, but it proved to be too expensive for them. However, to Charlie's delight, his mother (Maria) would be there.

This was to be Maria's second visit to the US, only this time she would visit Hollywood.

Charlie loved his mother and he proudly took her on a tour of all the studios he worked for, as well as all the various famous Hollywood landmarks.

Charlie also has a great passion for motorcars, and he would happily pose by the side of them. His mother must have been very impressed with what her son had achieved for himself here in Hollywood.

While Maria was in Los Angeles, she met up with Stan Laurel's father (Arthur Jefferson) and his second wife Venetia, who were there visiting Stan.

Arthur Jefferson kept a dairy of the time Maria was there and he recalls that on the 17th November 1935, Charlie Hall called and took them to meet his mother.

On another occasion Charlie called in just before Christmas to present Arthur and Venetia with a Christmas pudding that Maria had made. And on 2nd February 1936, there was a service held at St. Paul's Cathedral, Los Angeles for the King of England (George V) who had died two days before. Unfortunately there were so many people at the service that Maria had to wait outside with Charlie's wife (Foxie).

Arthur and Venetia met up with the Halls for the last time on March 14th 1936. They were there to say their goodbyes to Maria who was returning home to Birmingham.

Stan Laurel's daughter (Lois) recalls Charlie's visit and also offers some interesting information about our 'Little Menace'.

This is what she had to say about Charlie, in an interview with Dave Wyatt. What is interesting about this interview, is that Lois claims that Charlie would sometimes have input into some of the Laurel and Hardy scripts. Also, as Laurel and Hardy films were filmed in sequence, Charlie would often hang around the studio waiting for his part in the film. This might explain why he appeared in some of their films twice ('Battle of the Century' and 'The Hoose-Gow').

**Dave:** Do you remember seeing Charlie Hall much when you were young?
**Lois:** Well I don't remember Charlie and his wife coming to the Bedford house. But when my father was married to Virginia Ruth and they lived in Cheviot Hills, they had quite a few parties – dinner parties, garden parties in the afternoons and barbecues on the weekends. And Charlie and Foxie would always be there (Foxie being a very affectionate name for their close friend). When my grandfather came over with his wife, my Auntie Ven, they spent from July 1935 to July 1936. Fortunately I have the day to day diary from when he was there, and many of the entries were how kind Charlie & Foxie were to drive them here and there, around town and down to the beach for tea. I believe they even made a trip to San Francisco. I believe they went on a train. Stan and Babe were doing an appearance in San Francisco and I think they all went up on the train. Then Stan & Babe had to get back to work and it looks like Charlie & Foxie drove my Auntie Ven and my grandfather back down the coast, to their apartment in Beverly Hills. They seem to have had a lovely, lovely time.

I remember Charlie on the set very, very often. He seemed to always be part of things and I expected him to be there. And he always made a fuss of me, not having children of his own, just like Babe did, and I just adored him. Until the end he visited my father quite often. I don't ever remember going to his home. They lived in the San Fernando Valley, but I do recall seeing him at the Cheviot Hills house, and at the studio a lot.

**Dave:** Did you get on well with Charlie?

**Lois:** Yes, I think I felt closer to him because he was more my size – well, than Uncle Babe was.

**Dave:** You didn't have a problem with him, because you saw him being violent to your dad in the films the way Babe was in 'One Good Turn'?

**Lois:** (laughs) No, no, by that time I knew it was all put on and more like play. It was all written, and they really did adore everybody, and it was just in the story that they had to do these violent things; if you want to call them violent.

**Dave:** What did you think of Charlie in the films?

**Lois:** I thought he was very funny. Just about as funny as my father or Babe. And it just seemed right that he was a part of the family, so to speak, in the films. You expected to see him, and disappointed when you didn't, you know.

**Dave:** Did you see Charlie when he was doing other work at the studio?

**Lois:** No, it was more when he was acting. But even if he wasn't working that day, he was around. They never knew how far they were going to go in the filming that day. So they'd cover themselves by having everybody ready in case they went on to the next scene.

**Dave:** Did you get the impression Charlie was involved in helping on the scripts?

**Lois:** Oh I think so. I can remember my father saying, "What do you think of this?" to Charlie at home. They'd have gag sessions and there'd be Charley Rogers and Charlie Hall and my dad. And then they'd bring in the gag writers that didn't come to the home. Charlie would be at the house, but also on the set. Before they shot every day they would huddle together, and work out what they were going to do, to a point – they didn't always come about the way they planned. Something unexpected might come up, and then they'd all laugh and they might decide to do it that way. Yes, I think Charlie Hall contributed tremendously to the stories and scripts.

## The Bohemian Girl and Our Relations

Strangely in the Laurel and Hardy film 'The Bohemian Girl', Charlie doesn't make an appearance but you can hear his voiceover offering congratulations to Stan.

*Charlie's mother on the set of 'The Bohemian Girl'.*

At one point in the film, we hear Stan say, "Have a cigar."

"What's this for?" (Charlie's voice).

"Ollie's just had a baby."

"Oh, congratulations," (Charlie's voice again).

"Thank you," says Ollie.

Then, in 'Our Relations', Laurel and Hardy walk past a pawn shop. Their twins (Bert and Alf) are in the shop. Charlie can clearly be seen working in the shop, but he doesn't have any lines to speak.

## *Chapter Ten*

# CHARLIE RETURNS TO BIRMINGHAM

In 1937 Charlie Hall decided to return to Birmingham. He made the trip alone. The reason his wife (Wilda) was not with him remains a mystery.

His mother was very ill at the time, and this may have been the purpose for his visit (his sister Florence had also made a visit to see his mother just a year before).

One or two members of his family believe there was another reason he came home. They claim he was suspended from the Hal Roach Studios, for not turning up on the set. This, according to his family, was due to nights out drinking with Stan Laurel.

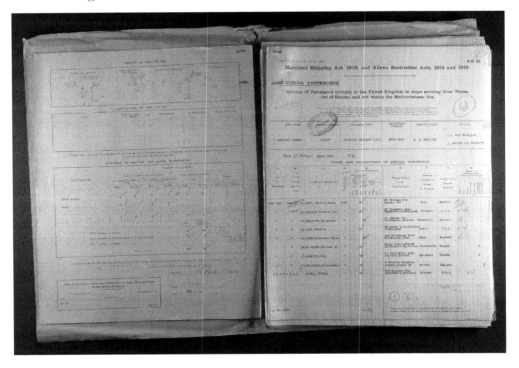

*Charlie returns to Birmingham 1937.*

Stan Laurel and Charlie Hall would often socialise together, and Charlie spent many a happy hour on Stan's boat fishing for marlin. Around this time Stan Laurel's contract with Hal Roach had run out, and he was refusing to sign a new one. Oliver Hardy's contract still had two years to run and there was talk of this great comedy team splitting up.

So perhaps Stan had a bit of spare time on his hands, and spent some of it drinking with his English 'buddy' Charlie.

Also some members of Charlie's family made an astonishing claim that Charlie married a second time, and came to England to get away from the trouble he was in. They believe that this is the reason Wilda was not with him.

However, Jean Cook (Charlie's niece) remembers it differently. She claims that after another heavy night's drinking (with Stan) Charlie woke up one morning in a motel, and found a marriage certificate stuck to the mirror. He indeed thought he had married a second time, only to find that he was on the end of a prank instigated by Stan Laurel!

*Jean Cook (on the right) with Bryan and Rachel Hall.*

Whatever the reason, Charlie Hall was on board the passenger ship 'The American Farmer' sailing to England alone. Lloyd French, who worked as an assistant director for 14 years at the Hal Roach Studios, was there to see him off.

While on board 'The American Farmer', Charlie wrote one of many letters to his good friend, film

*The American Farmer. The ship Charlie returned to England on in 1937.*

director, George Stevens. George Stevens was one of the most talented and respected filmmakers the world has ever known. He was nominated five times for an Academy Award as best director, winning twice. He was responsible for many classic films such as 'Gunga Din' (1939), 'A Place in the Sun' (1951), 'Shane' (1953), 'Giant' (1956) and 'The Diary of Anne Frank' (1959).

Charlie first met George when he joined the Hal Roach Studios around 1921-22. He began there as an assistant cameraman, but soon made his way up to director of photography. George Stevens was involved in many of the Laurel and Hardy silent comedies, as well as a few of their talkies.

He directed The Boyfriend series for Hal Roach, before moving to RKO circa 1933. It is often said that George Stevens 'took' Charlie with him to RKO.

So as we are about to see (letter one), Charlie Hall began writing to someone who was to become very important indeed. This letter (in the form of a diary) still survives and it shows how quickly he takes on the role of 'The Little Menace'.

It's an incredible letter that proves that Charlie did in fact 'like a drink', and he would take on the role of another character if he became annoyed. As we can see from the envelope he posted the letter upon arriving back in Arley Road, Birmingham.

The letter shows Charlie at his menacing best. His frustration is obvious and it seems he became bored very easily. The last part of the journey sounds horrendous, with the ship withstanding a battering from the sea.

After enduring this terrifying experience, life back in England would soon turn sour for the little man from Ward End.

Letter one.

AMERICAN · MERCHANT · LINES

On Board S. S. *Charlie Mar 15th*

Dear George thanks for all your kindnesses, Boat was late two days, so did not leave New York until Sunday evening, scared stiff the menace would show up any minute. Well I made it.

Lloyd French came to the boat to see me off, he did a very good job of it, we were doing alright, he fainted just before sailing time, did not want to be alone, called head steward and Purser, slipped steward couple of mickeys, there is a dame on board, a little bit of alright, steward promised to put her at table with me, he fainted cause he had to reserve seats for dinner, meantime met the Pilot we had a couple, hope he makes it out to sea.

To dinner, steward double crossed me, ask table steward to bring him over, he just laughed, said not to night,

*Letter one contin...*

2/

he is passed out, had dinner so to bed.
A little hangovery this morning eye opene
Shower, Shave, to breakfast, their
are only 18 passengers aboard, but
where's the young dame.

Sitting in Lounge getting dirty looks,
here comes the head Steward "What the
hell did you put in those drinks" I
thanked him, for putting me with the dame,
he said dont mention it, I told him the news
he said he did not remember leaving my
cabin, and that he was on the carpet this
morning, for neglecting the passengers.
Very Foggy— Fog horn blowing continiesly,
otherwise not bad going, nothing exciting
bar open - pick me up, dull day, no one
talks Im in the dog house, "So Nuts",
few nips before dinner, one eye from the
angry mob, dinner, listen to the radio,
so to bed.                          Mar 16th
Looks just like its going to be just another
day at sea, have not seen Princess Charming
"Ha, here she comes, in all her glory, little

*Letter one contin…*

3/.

pale but interesting, she spoke, here we
go "Wow" Giggling Gertie, elderly dame
enters, "Mother" its the main one that gave
me the one-eye, play a little menace
any how till lunch, think I'll tell a little
risky story, laughs just the same, may
just as well talk sense that will probabl
panic her, = Lunch = Mother and Gertie
dissapear, she's probably in the dog house,
a couple of nips, to dinner am going to
put on the dog for the rest of the trip, I'll
learn these frozen nutted limmies.

Mar 17th

17th Of Old Ireland, what a day for a rib,
I'm posing as an American, Purser, chief
steward are in on it, we're off, chap asks
where I'm from in the States, California,
the grandest place on earth, well that
started it, got into it good and heavy, few
collected around, a ribbers paradise all
biting good, I'm in fine fettle, we compare
England and U.S. finer schools, colleges,
fresh vegetables, flowers year around,
trains, automobiles, how many people own
cars or even rode in one in England.
Snobby English, relax, be human, keep
the poor down, no chance for opportunities.

*Letter one contin…*

4/.

England makes good clothes, yes but don't wear them, cain't afford to, have to send them to U.S. all English I know are baggy pants never send clothes to cleaners, change underwear once a week, never take a bath homes in U.S. much better, just one class of people there, you can talk to a millionaire just as easy as a street cleaner, women are more beautiful, go to beauty salons the English, no, God knows they need too, they asked me why did'nt I stay in U.S. if I dislike England and English so much, "thats the bull-headed English for you", here we are just comparing notes, and you get sore about it, they start to apologize, cain't let them do that, the fun will be over. So I told them I kind of resented that last crack, that I would probably take one look at the weather, crummy people, dirty buildings, traffic on wrong side of the street, English that cain't talk their own language either have a plum in their mouth, cockney accent or Lancashire dialect, one needs an interpretor, only one spoke the King's English and they fired him for doing it, Edward VIII. then we got on the Simpson subject, it would require hours for me to write it all down.

*Letter one contin…*

5/1        George "

# AMERICAN · MERCHANT · LINES

On Board S. S. 5 oclock

Pardon me Ladies and Gents, have to get
ready for dinner, little bath you know,
only had a shower this morning, the reason
the crack, steward told me some of them
had not taken a bath yet. = Tuxedo =
a little late for dinner, grand entrance, had
a couple of snorts, see the takem's of me
wearing Tux, they wont talk, so I brought
up the War debt who won the war, one
lady is going to report me to the authorities,
I order limberger, there they go.

Mar 18th

Here I am walking around like a leper,
they all scream when they see me coming,
the only ones that talk to me, Purser, steward
bartender. Wish you were along, need a
little support. Picture show tonight,
notice up for Life Boat Drill tomorrow.

Mar 19th

Life boat drill, rainy and foggy, hope
they do it between rain drops - for

*Letter one contin…*

6/

protection I'm wearing Sou-wester that I borrowed from a 6ft steward, this is not a weather permitting call, stewards hollering all on deck, doing Don Juan routine with fire hoses, Whistle blowing - bells ringing, everyone with a life belt on, couple of men wearing derbies, one woman so excited you would swear it was on the up and up - we all dash to our life boats! Girtie is all screwed up, arms, legs around an officer's neck wishing something would happen, wants to play this game every day. - I'd like to play but this is not the game - or the place to play it - wonder if she will ever wise up - like to take her to my cabin, give her a little fatherly advice or throw a drink into her or something."

Mar 20th

"Ahoy There", Ahoy", what ho me lads and a bottle of rum" = Thar she blows, the old Tub creaking and groaning - don't blame her, I'm doing a little myself, - and I'm not alone - furniture busted"

*Letter one contin…*

in corners with ropes, sailors dashing around, crashes all night, pitched tossed rolled all around, how long the Tub will stand it I don't know, sounds like a Roach breakaway, just waiting for Johnny Murray to pull the wires, rolled out of bed several times, decide to stay up, I'm not alone, women crying, the sober men not doing bad, no one allowed on deck — all doorways bolted, waves covering ship, Christ how she ploughs through them, rail washed away — going to get stiff, a bottle of Scotch bartender, have a nip — can't right now catch it on the fly later, that bastard sea she can raise hell — you're powerless, I'm going to get stiff, if she goes, won't know it — "Ahoy me Lads and two bottles of Scotch", Thar she blows and blows, the old tub crying its eyes out, has plenty of company,

*Letter one contin…*

8/.

rolling around like a drunk on a drunk on Subway Express — Stewards hollering if you want any food or coffee, go to the dining room — another couple of snorts I'll be there — refuse to starve to death — even if the boat does go down — dining room — has one table with frame around — so food won't go in your lap — six of us make it — order food and coffee, no table cloth, just knifes, forks and spoons — waiter brings food — spills half down passenger's necks — I'm one of them chairs sliding all around — food coffee all over table — Christ what a routine — everyone and thing all over the joint — we get each others food — glad to get it — No beefs — we're all Pals now — "The American Farmer — you have to be a dumb bastard to take this boat — this time of the year — hope I get this in the mail then I know I'm O.K.

This is all for now

Charlie "

*Letter one contin…*

Charlie's next letter to George Stevens is dated April 14th 1937 (letter two). There is no address on the top, so he may have been staying in London.

Charlie
April 14 - 37 =

Dear George

How about a pick me up.
Enclosed you will find a trade paper report on "Quality St.", when it opens will try and get the London daily papers report on it.

Things are awfully slow in the picture game here, only six shooting, they have some grand Studios here and well equipped but they don't know what to do with it.

Saw Otto Ludwig, he wishes to say hallo to you and Fred Guiol, he treated me fine and got me a good interview with Sonnie Hale, may get something in his picture.

By the way I have a date near London at the Theatre Royal, Chatham, to do an act May 3rd, hope last through the week, anyhow I won't send my laundry out till Tuesday. Have a lot of good agents coming to see it, so it had better be good, for that's my only solution. Tell Jack as yet have not found Lloyd Hacklett, will George

So Long
Charlie

*Letter two.*

94

George Stevens directed the film Charlie is referring to 'Quality Street' and it starred Katherine Hepburn. It was released in the US on 26th March 1937.

Charlie also mentions Sonnie Hale, who was in the UK directing the film 'Gangway'. However there is no record of Charlie appearing in the film.

Did Charlie fulfil his date at The Theatre Royal? Unfortunately there are no records to say one way or the other (incidentally, the Theatre Royal, Chatham was demolished in 2009, despite a spirited campaign to save it).

The next letter from Charlie to George Stevens (letter three) is very interesting. As we can see, Charlie was staying in the Bedford Corner Hotel, in London.

Was Charlie Hall right? Did Charley Chase move to RKO? Yair Solan who runs the WORLD OF CHARLEY CHASE website tells us:

*"In 1937, a few months after Charley Chase began working at Columbia Pictures, Chase briefly acted as a special assistant to Pandro S. Berman, the producer of the Astaire-Rogers musicals at RKO, essentially acting as a comedy consultant. Chase was set to play Astaire's valet in the actor's first solo film after his work with Ginger Rogers, 'Damsel in Distress', which was to be directed by George Stevens, his former Roach studio colleague. Due to health issues, however, Chase had to bow out of the project, and George Burns and Gracie Allen were cast as Fred Astaire's comic relief in the film."*

And what about Charlie's astonishing claim that Hal Roach was in partnership with Benito Mussolini's son Vittorio. This is in fact true. Hal Roach and Vittorio Mussolini (who was in charge of the Italian film industry) planned to make Italian operas. The company would be called RAM (Roach and Mussolini). However Roach backed out after pressure from the film moguls of Hollywood.

Did Charlie go and see Hal Roach while he was in London? It seems unlikely, as I believe he would have mentioned it, in his other letters to George Stevens.

Charlie now spent some time with his family, many of whom were based in and around Birmingham. He made sure that he visited all his brothers including Walter who lived in Banbury, Oxfordshire. It seemed that Charlie was very close to his brothers, and as mentioned they were very proud of him. And who wouldn't be?

However Charlie's frustrations about life back home in England explode in this next letter to George Stevens (letter four).

Imagine working and living in Hollywood during 'The Golden Years' and now here he is back in his native city, with no money and no job! Once again he becomes 'The Little Menace' and this time the volcano erupts!

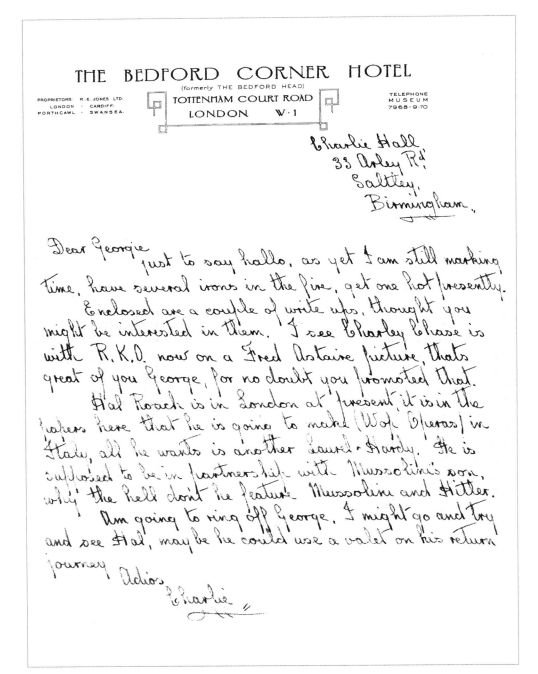

THE BEDFORD CORNER HOTEL
(formerly THE BEDFORD HEAD)
PROPRIETORS: R.E. JONES LTD.
LONDON · CARDIFF.
PORTHCAWL · SWANSEA.
TOTTENHAM COURT ROAD
LONDON    W·1
TELEPHONE
MUSEUM
7968-9-70

Charlie Hall,
33 Arley Rd,
Saltley,
Birmingham.

Dear Georgie just to say hallo, as yet I am still marking time, have several irons in the fire, get one hot presently.

Enclosed are a couple of write ups, thought you might be interested in them. I see Charley Chase is with R.K.O. now on a Fred Astaire picture, thats great of you George, for no doubt you promoted that.

Hal Roach is in London at present it is in the papers here that he is going to make (Wop Operas) in Italy, all he wants is another Laurel-Hardy. He is supposed to be in partnership with Mussolini's son, why the hell dont he feature Mussolini and Hitler.

Am going to ring off George, I might go and try and see Hal, may be he could use a valet on his return journey Adios,
Charlie

Letter three.

96

Charlie Hall,
33 Arley Rd,
Saltley,
Birmingham,
England,
Feb, 14th

Dear George just the usual "Hallo", and what have you, nothing much exciting to tell you. Motion Picture game still very quiet here. Weather as per usual, plenty of it good and lousy, have not seen the sun for over three months, matter of fact if you can see a hundred yards it is a clear day. The English papers are full of Stan and his wives troubles, they call him Englands comic "Henry the Eighth", he's doing alright for himself in the new year. Do you ever hear or see Dinah Duquette, just this morning recieved a letter from him and Margaret, they are living at Hermosa Beach.

Few observations of the English.

Mostly all have dirty noses, with a dew drop on the end, hardly ever use handkerchiefs, blow their nose by putting the finger alternately at each nostril, then blow, the idea is not to get any on your clothes. The first time I tried it was against the wind (not so good) they also have another nice clean habit taking snuff, yes girls as well. Their are some honey of dames here, they don't know the first thing on make up, walk around like clowns, their idea

*Letter four.*

97

2

of dress is terrible, and they think personal hygiene is something to eat. Stragly hair, earl Harbough eye brows, yes and hair under the arms, buck teeth mostly decayed and some missing, all have beautiful red noses with a strawberry finish. Their feet "Holy Christ," are these dames bad on their feet, Garbo and Chaplin combined, they really fuck em up and lay em down. Stockings, generally cotton all wrinkled. God knows what their bloomers look like, I know I would hate to be a fair. As for a bath they only see one when they see a De Mille picture, and if you want some fun go to the pictures here. The S.B. are eating from the time they get in to the time they leave and do they get their gabbing done. A few items of what they eat. Fish and chips, tripe, pigs feet, cow heels, chillings, baked potatoes, oranges, bannanas and what have you. Oh yes, must not forget you can also beg a cup of tea, which is great fun when you are trying to follow a picture someone hollers for tea, then you have to go through a routine of passing it along, same with the money, then the change.

Went to a football game, attendance is around 60,000 at the average game, prices 25¢ they all go half tanked up on beer and you know how beer effects you, well they all piss where they are standing, and it makes no difference if there is a lady around, if you have a

*Letter four contin…*

98

girl friend with you, just be Gentleman enough to move over a couple of places and let go by someone elses friend. at half time it looks like the 'Johnstown Flood.

Barber's charge 12 for a hair cut, their idea of a hair cut here is to run the clippers all around the sides and back, just leaving a tuft of hair, like a piece of grass, shape of a saucer, they all look like stooges, I'm not kidding, more comics running around with big muffs, derby hats and tandem bikes. To get on a Bus or a street car is just like being in a dog kennel, they take their dogs along wherever they go, it is nothing to see a dozen dogs in one bus at a time, first thing you know one starts barking, then they're all off, probably finish up with a fight, yeah the guys as well.

All stores are closed by eight oclock at night, you cant buy cigarettes or nothing. Pubs close at ten p.m. cant buy no more booze then until 10,30 A.M. next day, so if you have a hangover its just too bad.

Well George, I am coming to a close "What did you say?" "Thank Christ", adios

Yours Sincerly
Charlie Hall

*Letter four contin…*

On the second page of letter four Charlie mentions about going to a football game. But which team did Charlie support? Birmingham has two major football teams. They are Aston Villa and Birmingham City. There is a great rivalry between the clubs, and I have been a season ticket holder at Aston Villa for many years.

Charlie talks about going to a game, where the average crowd attendance is around 60,000. This can only mean that Charlie Hall went to watch Aston Villa in 1938.

On February 16th 1938 (the day before Charlie wrote letter four) Aston Villa played Charlton Athletic in a replayed F.A. Cup tie. The first game had ended in a 1 – 1 draw. The attendance for this game was 61,530 and once again the game ended in a draw. Eventually Aston Villa would beat Charlton (4 – 1) but they lost in the semi-final to Preston North End.

This may suggest that Charlie was in fact an Aston Villa supporter. Having said that, many people at the time would go to watch Birmingham City one week, and Aston Villa the following week. This practice stopped when watching football became too expensive.

Incidentally, the manager of Birmingham City in 1938 was a certain George Liddell. I mention this because George Liddell was later to become the headmaster of Charlie Hall's old school, Leigh Road.

Did people really pee where they stood, as Charlie said? Unfortunately the answer to this is yes! I have seen this done, during my time watching Aston Villa during the seventies. In fact it was quite common at most football grounds. You would be packed in like sardines and trying to get to the toilets was almost impossible, so some people would just urinate where they stood! And what about his description of the women of that era? Not very flattering at all is it? But I think the less said about this, the better!

It's now 14th March 1938 and this next letter shows how desperate Charlie has become. He is virtually begging his old friend George Stevens for money, so he can return to the US (letter five).

According to Charlie's family, he also went around to all his brothers and asked them to lend him money, for the same reason.

It's hard to believe that barely 12 months after appearing in the Fred Astaire and Ginger Rogers film 'Shall We Dance', Charlie was now working in a gas mask factory back in Birmingham.

His pledge of not taking a drink or buying a car, until he has repaid his debt smacks of desperation. And as you can see he has underlined some words to stress their importance. However he was soon to receive some good news and help, from one of his old friends from Hollywood.

Charles Hall,
33 Arley R'd
Saltley,
Birmingham,
England.
Mar, 14,

Dear George,
yes its your public pest No I, you were right when I made that loan before leaving of a 100 dollars, "Its a long way to go for a job on 'speck'. Well I have not been able to do a days work in pictures, for their really are'nt any being made, but I have been working in a Gas Mask factory past few weeks at the large salary of £3, 12, 6ᵈ. per week which is equal to about 17 dollars, and that seems to be my destiny if I remain here, of course they retire you when you are sixty five and give you the large sum of 2½ dollars per week for life. Well George I am appealing to you for another loan of 200 dollars, to help me

*Letter five.*

101

until I get going again back in Hollywood, if you will be kind enough to do me that favor, I promise to repay you on a monthly basis, will not take a drink or buy a car until I have repayed you this I promise. If you feel that you would like to loan me the money, you can deposit it with the "Thos cooke" officess they will transfer it here. I can then get a freighter passenger boat from London to New York, once I get to New York I don't give a damm I can walk it, or at least the old thumbing routine. The reason I tell you this, if you don't feel like you can afford 200 maybe you would loan me 125 dollars that would pay my fare to New York with a few dollars to eat on while trekking across to Hollywood.

I feel like hell having to ask you George but I really don't know of anyone better to ask, thanking you for all past favors, I am

Yours Sincerly
Charlie Hall

*Letter five contin…*

## Chapter Eleven

# WILL HAY AND BACK TO THE U.S.A.

Charlie Hall's old pal from the Hal Roach Studios (Edgar Kennedy) was in the UK to make a film with Will Hay, called 'Hey Hey USA'. Will Hay was a big star in England, and he was keen to 'crack' the American market. So to help him, the studios brought in a star from Hollywood, none other than Edgar Kennedy. Edgar managed to get Charlie a part in the film, and Charlie writes again to George Stevens to tell him the news (letter six).

As a matter of interest, George Stevens did in fact go on to direct the film 'Gunga Din' which starred Cary Grant, Douglas Fairbanks Jr., Joan Fontaine and Sam Jaffe who played Gunga Din.

It has often been said that from time to time Charlie Hall would take on the role of a 'cockney character', and this next letter proves the point beyond any shadow of a doubt (letter seven).

"Cor criky" Charlie seems more upbeat, and who could blame him, for he was now working in films again.

Charlie mentions he was paid "75 bucks a day" for his part in the film. This would pay for his fare back to the USA.

It seems a bit ironic that in the film 'Hey Hey USA', Charlie plays an American gangster. So we have an Englishman who would love nothing better than to be back in the US, playing a gangster in the US!

Charlie's part in the film is only very small. He plays a character called 'Lefty'. We first see him in what you would call a typical gangster's outfit, with a drink in one hand and puffing on a cigar. He then has a sequence with his good pal Edgar Kennedy. It starts with Charlie walking past Edgar who plays another gangster called 'Bugs'.

"Hello, Lefty," says Edgar.

"Bugs, gee it's good to see you again," Charlie replies.

Then after a brief conversation between them, Charlie explains he has to deliver a ransom note. At this point Bugs knocks him out. And Charlie's part in the film is over. In the letter, when Charlie says: "Ed and I went to the Darby", he means of course they went to Epsom to watch one of the biggest and oldest races in the world 'The Derby'.

Charlie Hall,
33 Arley Rd.
Saltley,
Birmingham,
England.

Dear George

How are you, have just had a very pleasant 6 hours with Ed Kennedy and his wife. Yes we finished up in a pub for dinner, etc, the "Lord Belgrave" Piccadilly Circus, too bad you and Dianna Ducat was not along to whoop it up a little.

By the way George received a letter from Art and Margaret this morning, they tell me they read in L. O. P's, column that you are going to direct "Gunga Din", which is to be a super, super special or something. Well thats great George and should you need someone to play Din just give me a ring.

Start with Ed on his picture, doing an American gangster, if I make enough dough don't be surprised to see me, what did you say, you don't want to, well adios

Charlie Hall.

*Letter six.*

Charles Hall,
33 Arley R'd
Saltley,
Birmingham,
England.

Cor-criky George you could have knocked me
down with a steam 'ammer, cor-sufferin
snakes, I'ave done three days work in
pitchers, with Ed Kennedy. Cor-stone
me up a gum tree, I got 75 bucks a day,
so cor strike me red, white and blue, I'll
be poppin in on you, and we'll have a
binder. Ed and I went to the Darby,
cor chase my aunt Fanny around the 'ouse
tops, it didn't 'arf rain, we were like two
pieces of blottin paper. Cor stuff me with
monkey nuts, a copper done a high-jump
fall stepped on a piece of orange peel and
cor strike me purple if Ed didn't tell him
to stop the clownin. Cor christ, we almost

*Letter seven.*

got pinched. The Director owns race-osses so 'e gave Ed and I 'is owner's passes, I 'ad to go as Mrs, Ed as Mr Varnell. Cor love a duck, I nearly got smacked on my ear at the owners gate, until I called my 'usband, 'e saved the situation. Cor sufferin snakes Ed and I were about the only two in lounge suits, cor strike me pink they were all runnin around in monkey suits, Grey toppers, carrying an umberella and a winder pane stuck in their eye to keep the rain out. Cor stuff me with water mellons, it looked like one of them big movie sets in 'ollywood only everybody were comics. Cor strike a light, said Ed what a sight to see, 'opes to be a seein you soon

Charlie Hall

*Letter seven contin…*

Charlie Hall
33 Arley Rd
Saltley,
Birmingham,
England
May 30th

Dear Georgie
your picture "Damsel in Distress", opened here yesterday. It is being well recieved, plenty of laughs and packing them in, enclosed is a write-up thought you might be interested in reading. Ed Kennedy told me to be sure and say hallo for him next time I wrote you, unfortunately we are having lousy weather right now, cold and rain but like the picture buisness it will be O.K. in a couple of months, adios
Charlie Hall.

*Letter eight.*

Charlie's last letter to George Stevens, from his home in Birmingham, was dated 30th May 1938 (letter eight). Europe was on the verge of war, but Charlie wouldn't be there to witness it. Instead he would soon be back in the US, and working with his good friends Stan Laurel and Oliver Hardy.

The film 'Damsel in Distress' won an Oscar for 'Best Dance Direction' for Hermes Pan.

At the end of 1938, Charlie said goodbye to his family in Birmingham, and set sail again for the USA. He would never return.

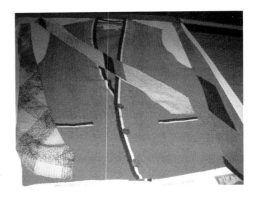

*Charlie's red waistcoat which can be seen in the Laurel and Hardy Museum, Ulverston, England.*

During his time in Birmingham, Charlie must have cut a dashing figure, dressed as he did in some of his bright clothes. He must have stood out like a sore thumb amongst the crowd, as he walked the streets of his home town. His waistcoat (now in the Laurel and Hardy museum in Ulverston) is bright red, and his relatives all have recollections of him in fluorescent socks, and flashy shoes.

Joyce Perry recalls that Charlie's mother was so embarrassed about his colourful socks and underwear, that when she used to hang them out to dry on the washing line, she would put them at the bottom of the garden, so that the neighbours wouldn't see them! So was this Charlie's normal dress sense?

Well Jean Cook seems to think that, once again, Charlie had fallen for a practical joke, played on him by Stan Laurel.

Laurel and Hardy had been in the UK in 1932 for a short tour, and Charlie asked Stan what people were wearing back in England. Stan replied that everyone was dressed in bright colours, so Charlie dressed accordingly.

*Joyce and Vic Perry.*

*Chapter Twelve*

# CHARLIE'S INTERVIEW WITH THE WEEKLY NEWS

Before Charlie Hall left the UK, he gave a very long and detailed interview about his life to the Weekly News newspaper. It is an incredible interview, and although not all of what Charlie says is entirely accurate, it is a fascinating story of our 'Little Menace' from Ward End in Birmingham, which covers the transition from the silent films to The Talkies, amongst many other things.

You can tell from the interview that Charlie holds Stan Laurel and Oliver Hardy with great warmth and affection.

**'THE WEEKLY NEWS' September '38**
"Probably the last thing in the world that Laurel and Hardy would have expected to achieve was the launching of a tune that would be almost as world famous as any other melody of all time.

That signature tune means just as much in the Federated Malay States and the Coral Islands of the Pacific as it does in the Orient or far flung Peru. It has also had the honour in America of being played as a National Anthem, when the band at a garden party were unable to get the music parts of the official anthem of an obscure Eastern ruler who popped in for tea!

I've been gagman to Laurel and Hardy, co-director – not forgetting the "menace" part in most of their films – for years and years.

You know the guy I mean – that tough piece of goods who usually appeared as the husband of the girl with whom Laurel has an innocent date because his own wife had gone with Hardy's to the pictures. (The same girl that Hardy was also making a pass at.)

All of this was at Hal Roach Studios, Hollywood, and some of the people who went through there and whom I am going to tell you about, include many of the great stars in their early days.

## THAT SIGNATURE TUNE

**To go back to the signature tune and how that came into existence. During the making of their first picture together, "The Battle of the Century", there was a young chap working around the studio named Marvin Hatley. Everywhere he went he whistled the same tune over and over again. This went on for several days, and at last Stan could stand it no longer.**

**"What the hell is that tune you keep whistling?" he shouted.**

**Marvin said he didn't know. Stan asked him where he heard it.**

**"I didn't hear it," he said. "It just came to me."**

**Just at that moment Hal Roach came in. Stan gave us the cue, and we whistled it in step with Hal's entrance. It made Hal laugh so much that we decided to use it as our trademark.**

And now I apologise for mentioning myself for a minute. I was just an interloping Englishman from Birmingham when I hit Hollywood, having gone there to try my luck in the great movie racket. I had to rough it going over, having just enough cash to make the trip and get through New York to the coast.

Hollywood was nothing but cornfields. I was terribly disappointed. I imagined a beautiful little place surrounded with a high wall. It was just the reverse. You were out in the wide-open spaces.

At that time Hollywood Boulevard, now the city's centre, was just a crossroads. I walked down towards Sunset Boulevard, and there was my first studio. "Lasky's". There was not much to it: just a wooden building.

Later that afternoon I saw my first Motion Picture Company at work. They were in front of a five-storey building. Everyone was sitting around talking, most of them sitting on the pavement, so I decided to sit by them and hear their talk. Much to my surprise at the time they talked like human beings. I found out they were from the Mack Sennett Studios and they were making a two-reel comedy.

After sitting around for half an hour, I asked one of the company when they figured on going to work. He told me they were waiting for the sun. I just laughed at him and said,

"Surely you don't expect the sun to come out any brighter than this?"

He said: "No. You see we have to wait until the sun is at a certain angle, then we go to work."

I asked him what was his job with the company, and what did he have to do. He told me that he was being co-featured with Slim Summerville, and that his name was Bobby Dunn.

He gave me an introduction to Slim. They told me to come to the studio next morning at 8.30 as they were using some extra people in their picture, and that I would receive the sum of £1 for my services.

I couldn't sleep that night for the thought of working in my first film.

I was up bright and early the next morning, and arrived at the studio at seven o'clock, being just able to gulp down some coffee, but too excited to eat.

Bobby Dunn invited me to the dressing room that he shared with several other comics: Andy Clyde, Jimmy Finlayson and Billy Bevan. Between them they made me up, put a moustache on me, and so to the set.

I did not do a thing all morning. I kept asking Bobby: "When do I get in front of the camera?"

Bobby sent me to the Director. I asked him. He gave me a funny look. I found out later that I was being framed, for directly after lunch I was called on the set.

The director asked everyone to leave the set as he was going to give me a test. He then placed me in front of the camera and told me to do something funny. I did not have to, for at that moment I was hit by mushy pies from all directions. Then everyone came from their hiding place and laughed.

The director told me to go round and get cleaned up, so I started for Bobby's dressing room. Just as I was about to go through a door another man came through in front of me, and the first thing I know he had a tub of water go all over him. The tub itself went over his head. This, I learnt later, was meant for me.

It struck me as very funny at the time. In fact I laughed till I cried as he struggled to get the tub off his face. Seeing me all alone and laughing, he naturally thought I had done it, for all the others had disappeared.

It was Mack Sennett, and also the termination of that period of employment.

## Slapstick Returns

The public taste runs in cycles. Crazy slapstick was the most successful humour for years in pictures. And in my opinion no heartier laughs are earned today anywhere than by some of the oldest of stock humorous situations.

And now we have Bill Powell and Myrna Loy going in for the slapstick of slapsticks in "Double Wedding".

A week later I got a job with Larry Semon, who then was the big shot comic of Hollywood. Larry, as you know, always made thrill comedies. This particular one had a streetcar sequence in it. I was to be one of the several passengers. We went off on locations and Stan Laurel was acting a comedy part in it.

Larry had a gag where Stan kept falling off the streetcar, and I will say in the course of two days Stan must have done fifty comedy falls. Oliver Hardy at that time was Larry Semon's "heavy".

### Stan Kept Babe In Stitches

He would watch Stan go through his routine and laugh immensely. So did I. Larry happened to see Babe laughing (Babe is Hollywood's name for Oliver Hardy) and asked him,

"What's funny now?"

Babe pointing at Stan said: "There's a funny comic if ever there was one; some day he will get somewhere in this business or I'm crazy. You had better watch out, Larry, or he'll steal the picture."

At the end of the second day when they saw the 'rushes', Stan got more laughs than Larry, so Larry went into conference with his top gag-men, and they decided to tie Stan to a telegraph pole for the rest of the picture as no-one can be funny tied to a telegraph pole for long! Stan, Babe and I got very friendly. And told each other our histories.

As you all know, Stan is English, left England in 1910 with the Fred Karno company. In the troupe was Charlie Chaplin and Fred Karno junior.

They got bad press notices in New York on their opening night, for the boys put on a new show, which they had rehearsed on their way over in a cattle boat.

Alf Reeves, Billy Reeve's brother, was managing the show. He is still with Chaplin as studio manager. He wired Fred Karno, and told him the show was a flop, and that the Press called them a "blithering, blathering bunch of Englishmen".

Karno wired back to get the scenery out of storage of the old stand-by, 'A Night in an English Music Hall', known in England as 'The Mumming Birds'.

The show went great and the boys played all over Canada and U.S.A. for several years. Finally it folded up and Chaplin went to Hollywood with Sennett at the enormous salary of £15 a week.

Stan found a partner and kept in vaudeville for a while. I always found him

*Hall Roach greets Fred Karno, as Stan Laurel watches.*

then a very unassuming little fellow, always ready with a laugh, with a grand sense of humour, very kind and always ready to help anyone. He is the same today and I can't imagine him anything else.

As for Babe, he was born in Georgia, U.S.A., played vaudeville, sang in a quartet and is a good singer. He first started in pictures in Florida, so you see he is a real pioneer. A grand fellow in every sense of the word, jovial and happy-go-lucky.

Little did we dream then that some day they would be a great comedy team, and that I would be an important part of their outfit.

## Disgusted With Films

We wished each other good-bye at the end of that short engagement and casually hoped some day we would work together again. Babe remained with Semon for many years. Stan made a one-reel picture called 'Mud and Sand', finally drifted back in vaudeville, for he was disgusted and very disheartened with films.

It was Charley Chase who brought Stan Laurel back to films. Charley had always been an actor, and had worked around U.S.A. and Canada in vaudeville for years. Like most vaudeville actors in America in those days he tried his hand at films and also, like most of them, he teamed up with Hal Roach.

Hal, seeing his possibilities, put him at once into one-reelers, and then promoted him to two-reelers. For twelve years on end he made eight pictures a year.

During Charley's reign as studio manager he saw Stan Laurel playing at the old Pantages Theatre in Los Angeles. He thought him extremely funny, and brought him up straight away to the studios for a test. Roach was of the same opinion and immediately signed him up for a series of two-reelers. They were not, however, a big success, and after the contract had expired, Roach did not renew his options. In those days Stan wore the usual comic clothes, ample and baggy, with his hair parted in the middle and well plastered down, having none of the individual style which is his today.

After leaving Roach, Stan signed up with Joe Rock. Joe is, of course, now making films in England, but in those days, he was working for Universal Studios in Hollywood. But Joe did not make the sort of films that Stan had been used to with Hal Roach, and therefore the few steps that he had climbed with Hal he now fell down, and in next to no time he was looking for a job.

## After The Same Job

I next saw Stan in the office of the De Mille studios, both of us being after the same job. Stan did not get the job, but I can't crow, because for that matter neither did I.

But you can't keep a good man down, and the next trip was back to Hal Roach where Hal was featuring Clyde Cook. Stan was then employed at £15 a week at the very studio where he latterly made £20,000 a picture. As luck would have it, Clyde did not like the director he was working under, and asked for a new director. Hal Roach asked Stan if he would take on this job. Few people are aware that Stan Laurel was a director in pictures long before he was a famous comic, but undoubtedly this experience had stood him in good stead in the making of some of their best efforts.

It was just at this moment that Clyde needed a heavy, and Stan's mind went back to the Larry Semon days. He immediately got in touch with Babe. After that he used him in all Clyde's pictures. They became firmer friends and have been inseparable ever since, until this rift broke their film partnership.

One day Hal was directing an all-star picture, and he asked Stan to step in, put on the grease paint and do a short routine with Babe. They worked so well on this, that Hal more or less wrote the next picture for them.

When the New York office saw that film they went wild with joy. It was the official start of the Laurel and Hardy team, for though they were actually to arrive as far as the public were concerned a bit later, a very important event was to happen before that.

It was the old stuff in a new setting. The Laurel and Hardy team has thrown thousands more pies and made thousands more laugh. Honest to goodness slapstick is welcomed by the general public.

Hal Roach was born at El Mira, New York, and migrated as a young man to Alaska. He owned his own truck. One day he had a job to deliver some goods to Southern California, and that gave him his first glimpse of people making pictures.

This, thought Roach, is decidedly more congenial than truck work, and he made up his mind then and there on the spot, that was going to be his business.

He promptly sold his truck and joined the staff of the Universal Studios as a stock cowboy at a salary of £5 per week.

## Harold Was A Cowboy

It was at the Universal Studios at that time that Hal Roach first met Harold Lloyd, who was also engaged as a cowboy on the lot.

With the money from the sale of his truck and some savings, he decided to become a film producer.

**I think the first film that Hal Roach made – all you needed at that time was one camera man, one assistant director and one prop man – was called 'Lonesome Luke'. It was a short comedy, and it was made with Harold Lloyd. The picture was sold, and Roach got a contract to make a series of the 'Lonesome Luke' comedies.**

At that time all comics were trying to be Chaplins. You know, with the baggy trousers, big broken cracked shoes, and the 'muff' which I should explain is the Hollywood name for a moustache.

And during this series of comedies happened an accident, which resulted in Harold changing his style altogether.

Harold was posing for some special 'stills'. He thought he had a property bomb in his right hand, and as the fuse burned merrily Harold was lighting a cigarette with the flame. Someone had let a real bomb that had been used as a pattern get in with the others, and it might have been a tragedy. It was only a light kind of bomb, but nevertheless Harold lost part of his hand, and it was during his convalescence that Hal thought of the new and sensational character who was literally to shake the film world.

It was this accident that produced the Harold Lloyd that we know. Hal discarded Lloyd's misfit clothes, fashionable to comics just then, and dressed him up smartly, at the same time covering up the disfigured hand with a rubber glove. He finished him off with those famous glasses that never had glass in them and gave him such stories as 'Grandma's Boy', 'Sailor Made Man' and 'Safety Last'.

I venture to say Harold has not made such good pictures since he left Roach. Everyone in the motion picture industry likes to work for Hal Roach. From top star to labourer, they're all his pals, and they feel that he is theirs. He maintains that each one is as vital as the other and that they are all part of the complete organisation, and all essential in their own ways to make good pictures.

He always pays top wages, and insists on closing the studios on Saturdays at noon. He gives a big party at Christmas and presents are distributed to his workmen and their families, and it was only right that during one of those parties Hal got the idea for the famous 'Our Gang' comedies.

It was like this! He noticed some kids playing together and could not help standing near them for quite a time listening to the conversation. It amused him so much because it was all so serious that he made up his mind on the spot that the public would enjoy such natural humour. Those kids were the original 'Our Gang' kids.

*Photo from Bryan Hall's collection.*

He told the fathers to have the wives bring the kids to the studios the next week, as he was going to make a film comedy of them. Everyone thought he was crazy, and as a matter of fact he almost went crazy doing it, but patience succeeded, and he hasn't stopped making 'Our Gang' pictures since.

Mickey, the freckled face kid, was a labourer's son; the father of Joe Cobb, the fat boy, worked in the office; Mary Kormand was the daughter of a photographer; the fathers of Sunshine Sammy and Farina were janitors. Hal personally plays Santa Claus to the Gang each year and hands them the presents.

The situation was that those kids were suddenly earning a lot more money than their fathers. But it hasn't disturbed any family relationship to my knowledge. Of course, kids will grow up, and, consequently, the Gang has changed quite a lot. For instance, Johnny Downs, now a juvenile lead at Paramount, was an 'Our Gang' kid 14 years ago.

Meantime, Laurel and Hardy were getting so well known, and, in fact, almost celebrities. They began to be invited to all sorts of public and private functions. Hospital and Christmas funds, dinners, premieres, and so on.

Nobody before or since, to my mind, suggested the perfect vamp like Theda Bara. She fairly oozed wickedness.

Mabel Normand was, of course, world famous in Chaplin successes and was featured in the first five-reel comedy called 'Tilly's Punctured Romance', a big success.

Lionel Barrymore was another great star whom Roach featured in a two-reeler, and believe it or not, I've seen that great and glorious actor do a fall into an ice cold fish pond at three o'clock in the morning.

Incidentally, Gary Cooper was an extra in that picture, getting thirty shillings a day, and without any thoughts of one day making 'Mr Deeds Goes To Town' and many others. What a man is Gary! One thing I can tell you. He is the same personality now than when he was as an extra. That's the test.

The ordinary stock girls at the Roach studio included: Janet Gaynor, Molly O'Day, Fay Wray, Olive Borden, Lupe Velez, Sally O'Neill, Jean Harlow and Sally Rand. Sally was not doing the famous fan dance then.

Should there be anybody who does not know exactly what that is, it is a dance in which Sally's only protection from the cold, cold elements is a fan which, ingenuously moved about to all her movements, provides at the right time adequate clothing (more or less!).

Beautiful Fay Wray's first job in pictures was doubling a cross-eyed comic who was acting the character of a bootlegger in a café sequence, dressed as a cigarette girl.

They used Fay for the long shots because of her pretty figure and handsomely neat legs. They also used a lion in that picture, and when she first heard it was to be included, was she scared? She thought they were joking, and I truly believe she didn't sleep a wink all night.

Her scare was nothing to mine. I had to take the part of an artificial lion that was always getting mixed up with the real one. I imagined that at any time it might take a too active dislike to my face.

Jean Harlow was always the best of troupers. She seems to have been pursued by some unfortunate destiny right from the beginning, and it is all the more tragic that, with it all, her personality was one practically continuously bubbling over with cheerfulness and courage and laughter. I know how much her cheerfulness is missed on the M.G.M. set.

Hal Roach, by the way, releases his pictures through M.G.M., and I think that I am right when I say that they made the first colour picture starring Lawrence Tibbett, the famous baritone of the Metropolitan Opera House, New York. This was directed by Lionel Barrymore. Laurel and Hardy supplied the comic relief.

Stan and Babe were always very loyal to their own gang, and more or less the same lot have been in their pictures as when they started. When M.G.M. wanted them for this picture, they took their own little crowd along and worked on the M.G.M. set as their own unit.

The film was eventually shown for its premiere at the Grauman's Chinese Theatre, Hollywood. A premiere in Hollywood means providing a show in a theatre, with searchlights all round it, at ten times the price that you would usually have to pay. There are thousands of people waiting on the sidewalks for a glimpse of their favourite star.

When Laurel and Hardy got back from San Francisco to Hollywood, Hal Roach had hit on another of his brainwaves. We were to make Spanish, French, and German versions of all our films.

Hal has a schoolroom on the lot that he uses for the "Our Gang" kids and this was turned into a night school, and the sight of Stan, Babe (Laurel and Hardy) and I sitting at kids' desks doing our lessons would have delighted Laurel and Hardy fans. The teacher wrote the words on a blackboard, and we copied them out on to our paper and then rewrote them as they sounded to us.

One day Stan nearly caused a riot by raising his hand and saying, "Please teacher, may I leave the room?"

This schoolroom scene provided the idea for the opening sequence in the picture that followed. It was the convict story you probably remember. A burlesque of "The Big House". (The film Charlie is referring to is 'Pardon Us'.)

**"In The Can"**

It was originally designed as a two-reeler, and, before we knew it, we had "in the can", as they say, more than the required length of showable film. Everything seemed to come out well, and to start a lot of ruthless cutting would spoil the continuity of the film. Stan went into conference with Roach, and they decided to make it into a featurette, which is a three-reel picture or just over. We completed it, and when it was finally cut (edited) it was found to be just over four reels, which is too long for a featurette and too short for a feature. More headaches. Hal Roach, Stan, and Babe ran it over and over in the projection room, and were unanimous that it was too good to take any scenes out, because it was a riot from beginning to end.

It could not be cut without spoiling, so Roach decided to make a feature of it, which he did, and that's how Laurel and Hardy got into full-length feature pictures.

Some of the best fun we had was in the making of 'Hollywood Party'. In this film, Lupe Velez had a tremendous egg-sequence with Laurel and Hardy.

While the picture was being made, Lupe, Stan or Babe would start talking to different people on the set while another slipped an egg to a pocket. The appropriate tap would soon be obligingly delivered, and not a day passed without broken eggs being cleared out of somebody's pockets.

In this connection I have always admired the story told about Enrico Caruso, the great tenor. He and Scotti, the baritone, were always playing practical jokes upon each other during the actual performance of the opera.

There is a particularly dramatic moment in the opera, 'The Force of Destiny', by Verdi. Before they sing their big duet, 'In this solemn hour', they have to shake hands, and Scotti had to hide his embarrassment one night when he found that in the palm of his hand Caruso had placed an egg, and as the duet began they were both clasping a most unholy mess!

When a Laurel and Hardy film is being 'shot', it's our boast that it would be in the film and not on the cutting-room floor.

Laurel and Hardy do not shoot unnecessary feet of film, neither do they have five or six retakes of any one scene like many established and famous directors have to do. If anything, they're exaggeratedly careful. They don't go before the camera until they're absolutely certain they've got every bit of comedy out of that particular scene.

**It Really Is Mud!**

It is interesting to know that Laurel and Hardy always use the real things to get the full effect. Pies, cakes, cheese, honey, flour, whitewash, oil, vases, chairs, lamps, and pianos, and even mud holes. Only the genuine article need apply.

I ought to tell you about Laurel and Hardy's hobbies.

Stan is a real stay-at-home, and likes to fuss round the garden and greenhouses for hours and days on end. He's won medals for amateur gardening, and grows all his own vegetables.

Babe has a large chicken farm, where he spends a lot of the time that he isn't either working with Stan or away on one of his marvellous trips into the wilds of the country living the real simple life, and maybe he was getting one back on Stan when he told him that he was feeding his hens on tomato ketchup so that they would lay seasoned eggs.

Stan is still about as British as anyone could possibly be, in his home, his style, and his dress. He eats bacon and eggs for breakfast, and this with roast beef and Yorkshire pudding and lamb and mint sauce comprises his favourite trio of meats. He drinks gallons of tea, and finds it a great inspiration.

He's crazy, too, on deep-sea fishing, and has just about the fastest boat there is around those waters. His fishing equipment alone cost over £2000, but if you could see it you'd realise that it was worth every penny. We have trawled together for days out on the glorious Pacific Ocean, around Catalina Island.

**You Wouldn't Believe It!**

The expensive tackle is for swordfish, and if you haven't seen pictures of the swordfish they catch over there you'd never believe me when I say that last year he got one that weighed over 200lb.

You may have heard some tall fishing stories in your time, and I know that you've heard of the immense tunny that are caught over here, but Stan Laurel with a 200lb swordfish on the end of his line is a sight worth seeing.

It took him almost two hours to land it. No one is allowed to assist in the catch because it would mean disqualification from the contest for the medal that the Catalina Yacht Club present.

To land that fish you have to be strapped in a swivel chair with your fishing rod, in a harness, which is attached to you. In no other way would it be possible to get those hefty monsters.

Stan can never get over his longing to clown about and kid people, but in spite of this he is always kind and considerate, and his jests at the expense of others are always playful ones. He is ready at any time to help others, and has a great regard for the under-dog.

Both he and Babe abominate hypocrisy of any kind, and have no hesitation in holding it up to ridicule.

To look at him on the screen you wouldn't think he had an idea in his head, but believe me his mind is racing on all the while, and in my opinion there isn't a brainier comedian in the business.

One of the big secrets of the success of Laurel and Hardy was harmony. Neither one cared a scrap who got the laughs as long as the picture did. They're just the same now as they were when they were nobodies, as far as their personalities are concerned.

## Visit To Britain Amazed Them

England and Scotland, you will remember, gave then a great reception when they came over for a visit, and gramophone records were made of their signature tune. That trip amazed them, for up till then they had gone on content with the fact that their pictures had made the grade in a big way in America.

Babe's personality is of a different sort of 'easy goingness' to Stan's. Happy-go-lucky is the best description. He's a very early riser and always drives into the studio around eight o'clock. It makes no difference whether a picture's actually on the floor or not, he'll be there just the same. That's one of the routines that he does like.

He has a chauffeur, but almost invariably leaves him at the house, as he has an absolute passion for driving his own car with the radio playing.

The first thing he does when he gets in his dressing room is to switch on the radio as he reads his fan-mail.

And talking of fan-mail, don't listen to any stars who tell you that they're bored by their fan-mail. They're not. It's the breath of life to them, and if they get a million letters a day they'd not be bored. It's when they're getting nothing that they get bored, and then they're almost frantic to find out what to do about it.

Babe's a great cook, and loves to demonstrate this once in a while. You're lucky if you're in the house on one of those nights. He has his own special dishes, and when you look at them you realise why Babe's form would definitely not go even part of the way through the eye of a needle. Talk about tasty cooking. The only trouble is you eat too much, and you can't help it. He is very fond of company and hates to be alone.

## Study In Contentment

He is wild about fresh-water fishing, and hunting. This takes him often in the opposite direction to Stan on their vacations, and I've often gone away roughing it with him 'way up in the mountains'. That is definitely the life with Babe.

What appetites he has had to cook for up there on some occasions. To see Babe's expression just before breakfast time in the morning as he surveys a sizzling, grilling mass of meat is to behold an expression that you haven't found in any of his pictures ever. It's what I should call 'Study in contentment'.

*He is a good golfer, and when he's not doing any of the other things you'll find him in full cry at the Hollywood Lakeside Country Club, Babe's home contains without a doubt among other things, the very best bed I have ever had the pleasure of sleeping in. It's like going to sleep in a soft park, measuring as it does ten feet long by seven feet wide.*

One strange thing about Laurel and Hardy is that neither of them has ever been struck with the idea of wanting to be a great tragedian. Almost with exception the greatest comedians of the stage and the screen have at some time or other felt that they must make a big success in the greatest of tragic roles.

I think this is explained by the fact that in their business of making people laugh they get so keyed up to everything that is comic in life that a natural reaction sets in. They have to give vent to it in the expression of something deep, tragic and gloomy, and altogether different from the business of raising laughter.

The day that it is announced that Laurel is going to undertake the role of Hamlet I will travel from the far end of the earth and pay anything for a stall. The only rival to this, as an attraction to me would be Babe doing Macbeth at a neighbouring theatre.

## Musicals Preferred

Actually, the boys prefer musicals at the theatre. They can nearly always be seen on the opening night of every new show at the Biltmore Theatre in Los Angeles. This has housed the very biggest of the successful American plays. Babe is very fond, indeed, of going to the pictures and if he had to spend his time in the cities from morning to night watching films being continually run through in front of him he would raise no objections – that is, provided time for meals was comfortably allowed for.

Stan, on the other hand, enjoys nothing better than running the films through on his home projector. This is a first class machine, talkie and everything. He spent quite a fortune on it, and it has certainly repaid him when you bear in mind that he can borrow prints of the best pictures in Hollywood and just turn them through at his leisure.

Stan was born in South Shields, and finished his schooling in Glasgow. His father, Arthur Jefferson, was a performer on the stage for years, finished up as a theatre owner in Glasgow.

Stan went with Fred Karno's company at the age of 16, and years later he did not forget that it was Fred Karno who gave him his break. He gave Fred Karno Junior a job at the Hal Roach Studios in 1923.

In 1924 Fred Karno Junior took a comedy act on tour, and I was a member of the outfit. We went off to San Francisco, and our conveyance was one of those very old types of Ford, the sort that inspired that flood of 'flying bedstead' jokes that swept England and America some years ago. Talk about rattle!

The engine got very hot at one stage, and this caused the radiator to leak. Steam came hissing out of the radiator cap like smoke from an express train, until finally we had to pull up and call at a petrol station.

It was one of those American stations that are garage-grocery-store and chemist's shop combined. We asked them to fill up with oil and water, and while they were doing it we noticed the leaking radiator. It was just like a watering can. We could not get it fixed, and the garage owner seemed to know less about trouble than any of us.

Fred suddenly hit on a brain wave. He went into the grocery store and got three packets of breakfast food. This he put in the radiator. After a couple of minutes the leak stopped and off we went.

After going several miles we saw what we thought was snow passing by the windows.

*Charlie with Queenie Karno (Fred Karno Jr's wife).*

"That's funny," said Fred. "Here it is 90 degrees and snowing thick and fast. What do you know about that?"

It was so thick it covered our windscreen, and we had to stop and wipe it. We then found that the snow was Fred's breakfast food and it was pouring out of the radiator.

*We lifted the bonnet and saw a huge pudding. The engine was covered in it and in an instant so were we, for we had forgotten to turn off the engine. Stan later used this in one of his comedies.*

(Charlie is referring to the Laurel and Hardy film 'Hoose-Gow').

We eventually plodded on in that car to San Francisco and had the magnificent reward when we arrived there of finding that our contracts had been cancelled.

I came back to Hollywood and joined Hal Roach again. Fred went on, I think, to Canada. I haven't seen or heard anything of him since.

Later still, Stan found an interesting position for Fred Karno Senior, at Roach Studios and he was mighty happy to be in a position to do it.

## A Magnificent Schooling

The old two-reel comedies were a magnificent schooling for the stars of today. To mention just a few who were two-reeler people: Charlie Chaplin, Harold Lloyd, Will Rogers, Buster Keaton, Lloyd Hamilton, Wallace Beery, Lionel Barrymore, Gary Cooper, Bing Crosby, Gloria Swanson, Mary Pickford, Carole Lombard and Jean Harlow.

Frank Capra, who gave you 'Mr Deeds Goes to Town', 'It Happened One Night', and 'Lost Horizon', was just a gagman at the Roach Studios.

It is a very noticeable thing how popular British people are over in Hollywood. There's a large colony, and there's one thing you usually find about the members of it. In the main they keep outside more hectic Hollywood life, and settle down to a sort of 'Britain in Hollywood'.

Some of the finest writers over there have come from this country, and we know that this applies to actors as well.

There's a custom over in Hollywood to give a big feature a run through in the ordinary programme of a local suburban cinema, and there's no better way that I know of seeing how the public likes it.

On one memorable occasion after a Laurel and Hardy pre-view we were all so wrapped up in discussion about the picture that some of us quite forgot our wives, and left them in the theatre. We drove home without them – and it doesn't need me to tell you that we heard plenty!"

OK so we all know that Stan was born in Ulverston and not South Shields, but what about some of the other things, Charlie has said? I have asked Dave Wyatt to correct some other errors in his story. Here is what he had to say:

- 'Battle of the Century' wasn't Laurel & Hardy's first film.
- Charlie says he was at Sennett the same time as James Finlayson. This must have been in 1922 when Charlie first arrived in Hollywood. But not as he says, when Bobby Dunn "was being co featured with Slim Summerville", which was at least five years earlier. Then "a week later" he was with Larry Semon where Stan Laurel was doing a streetcar scene. There is no such scene in any of the three Semon films Stan Laurel appeared in, which in any case were made in 1918, before Charlie was in the country!
- The story of Laurel being tied to a telephone pole in a film "or he'll steal the picture" is usually attributed to Antonio Moreno, not to Babe Hardy. Hardy wasn't with Semon at the same as time as Laurel (his first film with Semon was the following year). The film was 'Frauds and Frenzies', perhaps Charlie heard and slightly confused the facts, or deliberately 'improved' on them to make them a better story? It is just possible that Charlie was referring to Stan and Babe being together on 'The Lucky Dog'. The January/February date would fit, with Babe about to start appearing regularly as Semon's heavy. Semon could have seen the rushes of 'The Lucky Dog' and heard the comment, that Stan was funny. And there are incidental streetcar shots with Stan in 'The Lucky Dog' (although he doesn't fall off a streetcar, and no passengers are seen). But the part of the story with Semon tying Stan to a telephone pole doesn't fit here.
- Chaplin didn't go to Sennett because the Karno tour folded. He was lured away by a hugely increased salary.
- 'Mud And Sand' was three reels, not one.
- Hal Roach signed Stan up first for a series of one reelers, not two.
- Charlie Hall suggests Stan's Joe Rock films were poor and unsuccessful, this is not true. He had a contract disagreement.
- Unlikely Stan would try for a job at De Mille studios, they hardly made short comedies!
- Neither £15 per week or £20,000 a picture sound possible salaries.
- Stan first directed Fin in 1925 at Roach, Clyde Cook was later.
- "Clyde needed a heavy, Stan immediately got in touch with Babe". Except that Hardy was already on the Roach payroll, and had been in one of the films with Fin, that Stan had directed earlier.

- "Hal was directing an All star picture and asked Stan to step in and do a short routine with Babe". This is untrue. 'Get 'Em Young' is the film where Stan stepped in and Babe stepped out through an accident.
- '45 Minutes From Hollywood' is the first film where they both appear, but in separate scenes.
- The first Harold Lloyd film wasn't 'Lonesome Luke', and Hal Roach's first film wasn't with Harold Lloyd.
- Lloyd's prop bomb accident wasn't that early, and it didn't inspire the change to the glasses character (this was years before) and Lloyd's idea, not Roach's. He had to persuade Roach to let him do it.
- 'Tillie's Punctured Romance' not "Tilly's".
- "Mary Kormand" should read Mary Kornman.
- "Stan later used this in one of his comedies" (The Hoose-Gow). However it was tried with Charlie in 'Bacon Grabbers', but cut.
- And finally Gray Cooper and Mary Pickford weren't exactly stars of 2 reel comedies.

Thanks Dave, I couldn't have put it better myself!

*Chapter Thirteen*

# FRANK HALL

As I mentioned earlier on in the book, Charlie Hall had six brothers and one sister. A great deal of information about Charlie (his school etc.) came from his younger brother Frank. Although sometimes he could get his facts mixed up, he was the main source of information.

Frank was the youngest of all the Hall brothers and he was born in 1913. He was the only member of the family who was not baptised in St. Margaret's Church. This was possibly due to the family moving to Arley Road, and the impending First World War.

I first met Frank around 1992 at a Laurel and Hardy 'Helpmates' meeting in Kent. I remember queuing up to get his autograph. He had himself become quite a celebrity with his friends from the 'Sons of the Desert'. I told him I was from Birmingham, and that I was starting a tent in

*John Ullah, Steve Smith, Frank Hall and Barrie Finney. This was when it was cool to have a moustache!*

his home city. The tent was to be called 'Laughing Gravy' in honour of his brother Charlie.

Frank was over the moon about the idea, and he came along to our first meeting, which took place at The Barn Social Club in Witton, Birmingham. He loved our meetings, as it gave him a chance to have a couple of pints of mild and a cigarette.

"Don't mention it to the wife," he used to say. "She thinks I've packed up." It could have almost been a line from a Laurel and Hardy film! His wife (Gwen) of course knew all about his smoking. She once told me that she knew all the secret places where he used to hide his cigarettes in their house.

I liked Frank and he liked to talk about his brother. He once told me that Charlie had appeared in several pubs in the city, getting up to 'do a turn' in several of them.

I was amazed, and I asked Frank if we could meet up one weekend, so that I could interview him in more detail. This was fine by him, and he invited me over for tea. However, a few days before we were due to meet, I received the awful news that Frank Hall had passed away.

However Frank Hall was interviewed around this time and here is his account of Charlie and a few other things as well:

*"We were all close as youngsters, and me and Charles were like good mates, y'know. We heeded our father, as children did in those days, and we never had the kind of luxuries we had today."*

Frank told how Charlie regarded himself as an actor.

*"It were a surprise, because he went there as a chippy, and he would be working, then someone would come along and say 'you, you and you' and they would find themselves in a crowd scene, in a shop, a street or something like that. I think they picked on Charles a lot because he was a bit small, and may have looked, y'know, kind of weak or something. They liked that kind of thing. Then he'd go back on the tools and forget all about it. And then he seemed to get the taste for it, and he was well made up when he saw his name on the film, up there on the screen, and it paid a darn sight more than chippying."*

Frank was asked about a ring he was wearing.

*"Yes, that's his ring, it came down to me, and I've been wearing it. It were in loads of films. Oh here we go again, go on then, try it on. Funny, all people want me for is to talk about somebody else, try his ring on and talk about old films. I wish people would ask me about me, I'm a person too, y'know."*

Frank went back to Charlie.

*"Well, y'know, he worked with 'em all, really. With Laurel and Hardy he said it was a lot of clowning about, and getting messy, although a lot of that stuff was fake, y'know,*

*a lot of shaving soap, dough, harmless for the most part. I think he admired Buster Keaton the most, because he was a stickler for detail. A perfectionist, you might say."*

When asked what Frank remembered most about Charlie he replied,

*"Well, he were just a brother, who went off to do something else. Good memories of our childhood – great memories really. Charlie was always a bit mischievous. I just remember him as a nice, gentle lad, who liked a good laugh and was pretty easy-going. But, I ended up as a council worker, and he ended up a film star. That's life."*

Finally Frank was asked "Was your brother called Charlie or Charley?"

*"My brother was called Charles."*

Iris Summers (a friend of the Hall family) knew Frank and Gwen Hall. She claims that Gwen was an orphan who worked on the railways, and Iris's parents took her in. This is how she got to know Frank Hall.

One day in 1938, Iris Summers and her brother (Ron) went to visit the Hall's house in Arley Road. She knew from Frank that Charlie had come over for a visit. (She thought that Charlie might be over with Laurel and Hardy!)

As she approached the house she saw three figures coming towards her, one of which was Frank. Iris turned to her brother Ron and said, "Ron, Ron

*Harry and Frank Hall in Blackpool 1936.*

look at the one in the middle, that's the film star." She was of course referring to Charlie.

Iris used to go and watch Laurel and Hardy at the pictures when she was young and since meeting Frank, she now recognised Charlie.

When Maria Hall passed away in 1939, the house passed on to Frank and Gwen. However, Frank was in the army, so Gwen spent most of her time with Iris and her family.

Upon seeing the photograph of Frank with his brother Harry (taken in Blackpool in 1936) Iris was amazed at Frank's clothes and especially his shoes. She told me that you couldn't buy clothes like that in England at that time. This would appear to suggest that Charlie either sent the clothes over from the US, or he gave them to his mother to take back when she came to visit him.

Just before the Second World War, Gwen and Iris went up to see Frank, who was stationed in Scotland. Iris recalls that Gwen was pregnant and she wanted to see Frank before he went overseas.

They stayed at a pen-friend's house in the Gorbals. The Gorbals was a slum area of Glasgow situated on the South bank of the River Clyde. The slums were cleared and replaced by high rise flats in the 60s, but the area still had a notorious reputation as a very violent place to live.

Iris recalls they shared a bed, and not long after she blew the candle out, Gwen let out a loud scream. Iris quickly re-lit the candle to find the bed was 'alive with fleas' (to get an image of this, watch the Laurel and Hardy film 'The Chimp'). Unfortunately they never got to see Frank as he wasn't allowed out, in case he gave away details of where he was being sent to.

Dave Wyatt also interviewed Frank, around this time, and here we get some information of the two brothers back home in Birmingham. It is quite clear from Dave's interview with Frank, that Charlie did have a drinking problem, and poor Frank was to suffer as well. So perhaps the story of Charlie being suspended is true?

**Dave:** When did Charlie Hall come back to see you?
**Frank:** Charlie came over in 1938 and stayed for 12 months. He was very small – he was only 5' 4". When he came here he had a car and he had a cushion to see out properly. But he never did much walking about. He used to say, "Where's the taxi?" – even to go about 200 yards. But he soon got out of that.

I remember once we all went to a pub in Bewdley. They had some outdoor games there – jumping, skipping – and he won one – the sack race.

I think he surprised himself. And he won a prize – a big pint jug with the pub's name on it.

We used to go out drinking together. By the time he'd been here 10 months he got short of money, so he went on to beer. I used to wait for him to come home, get dressed and go out together drinking – used to be out 'til 3 or 4 in the morning – on whisky all night; bring a bottle home with him and drink that as well. I used to have to be up for work about 6 a.m. which made it very awkward for me.

He went home – I was an alcoholic. I was picking a drink up and putting it down again. I was like that (shaking). It was stopping me from getting anywhere so I had to go into the army, and that cured me. It was very hard to stop after all that time. But it cured me. After that I didn't see him again.

**Dave:** Did he write and tell you about the films he was in?

**Frank:** He used to write 2 or 3 times a year, but he never mentioned the films. Never mentioned Laurel & Hardy or anything. It wasn't until about 4 years ago I knew about it – Laurel & Hardy and the Sons of the Desert. If he was here today, he'd be very surprised.

**Dave:** Can you say anything about his early life before he went to America.

**Frank:** Well I was only 6 years old when he left for America. He was 19 when he went. He used to work at the Metropolitan Carriage Works – he was a carpenter by trade. But he used to go to one or two variety shows in Birmingham. He went to America and worked in a canning factory at the start and got fed up with that, so he tried out as an extra in films. He sent for my mother and she went over for 12 months, so I was housekeeper then until she came home; had to cook meals. She had a fantastic time. She saw all the studios and film stars – and Stan Laurel's father and mother.

**Dave:** Did you see his films?

**Frank:** No, only after the War. I saw one or two – and on TV (now).

**Dave:** What do you think of Charlie as an actor?

**Frank:** I think he was a good actor in his way.

**Dave:** With Laurel & Hardy he was known as 'The Little Menace'.

**Frank:** He was different to that. He wasn't a menace at all.

**Dave:** Did you meet his wife?

**Frank:** My mother did. They used to call her Foxie. She acted with him once or twice. She and Charlie went to Stan Laurel's home – had photos taken there.

He wanted me to go out there with him – sell the house up, but I didn't, I wish I had done. The weather's better there. If you can put up with this weather you can put up with anything I think.

## Chapter Fourteen

# THE REST OF THE HALL FAMILY

Incredibly, it was not until the early 1980's that we discovered that Charlie Hall was in fact born in Birmingham. Bill Cubin, who at the time ran the Laurel and Hardy Museum in Ulverston, had by chance met Charlie's nephew at a wedding reception in Bath. It was from this meeting, we discovered that Charlie's brother Frank was alive and well and still living in Birmingham. The nephew Bill had met was Bryan Hall.

I first made contact with Bryan Hall in 2007 and we began exchanging e-mails, photographs and information about his family. Bryan was born in Erdington, Birmingham, but his family moved to Banbury when he was two years old. He is the son of Thomas Walter Hall (Charlie's brother).

In 2008, Bryan very kindly invited myself and my partner (Mandy Finney), to have lunch with him. Over a wonderful meal (beautifully prepared by his wife Ivy) we sat and talked about Charlie, and of their memories of him, as we passed around a bottle of port. (Bryan's son Nick was also present). Bryan now refers to us as 'Uncle Charlie's Fan Club'.

Joyce Perry was born in Selly Oak Hospital, Birmingham and lived at 28 Village Road, which was at the back of the Aston Villa Football ground. She told me that she used to charge sixpence to look after cars on match days.

"We used to make a fortune," she said.

Her father was Harry Hall, another of Charlie's brothers. As a child, she used to go to the local cinemas with her mom and dad to watch Laurel and Hardy films. Her mother used to tell her, "That's your uncle," but she says that her friends didn't believe her.

In her youth Joyce Perry was a member of the famous Birchfield Harriers Athletics Club in Birmingham. She was evacuated during the Second World War to Banbury, where her cousin Bryan used to live.

*Bryan Hall (right) with his late wife Ivy and his son Nick.*

Being in Joyce Perry's company is a wonderful experience, and although she moved out of Birmingham quite a few years ago, she still has a Brummie accent and that Brummie sense of humour.

I managed to contact Jean Cook around 2004 and she came along to one of our Laughing Gravy tent meetings.

Her father was Herbert Hall (Charlie's eldest brother) and Jean has provided me with some fascinating information about Charlie.

Here then are Charlie's family.

**Thomas Henry Hall** (Charlie's father) was born on 25th June 1873 in Bromsgrove, Worcestershire. He would always list his profession as 'labourer' (as was his father).

Joyce Perry told me that growing up she had 'posh shoes' and her mother told her that they were not cheap! The shoes were from her grandfather who was very fond of her.

A family story about Thomas is that while he was working down a hole, something fell on his head, and this accident would eventually lead to his death.

On checking the 1911 census it shows that Thomas was working in the sewers, making it possible that this story is true. He died on 22nd March 1930 at the family home in Arley Road, with his wife Maria by his side. The cause of death on his Death certificate reads due to 'cerebral thrombosis'.

**Maria Hall** (Charlie's mother) was a very stern looking woman. The family rumour is that the Reynolds (Maria's maiden name) originally came from Canada, and that they had Native American blood in them. We cannot verify this, but her features, and olive skin, suggest it could be true.

Bryan Hall spent a lot of time with her during the war. Her fierce looks frightened him, but he points out that she was in fact a very nice lady.

Iris Summers holds virtually the same opinion, and Joyce Perry remembers her as always being in an apron, and always being very busy.

Iris remembers the Hall's house in Arley Road, and told me that you always entered it via the back door.

She also recalls that next to the kitchen, the Hall's had had a bath fitted, and she used to go there to have a bath. This saved her from paying 2d at the local baths!

*A very stern looking Maria Hall.*

Iris claims that the house was very nicely decorated with nice furniture. "They were posh," says Iris.

This may mean that Charlie was sending money over to his mother, who Iris claims he loved very much.

So the working class Halls were now seen as posh!

"Maria Hall," says Iris, "was a very house proud lady."

"You have to remember I was only young at the time, and to me she looked like a very stern woman, rather like Queen Victoria. However she was a very, very, kind lady, very reserved and very quiet. A bit like Frank."

Bryan Hall confirms what Iris said about the house in Arley Road: "You always entered it from the back. You weren't allowed to go in through the front door."

This was a very common practice. Growing up as I did in the sixties, we would also enter our house through the back door.

Maria Hall made two trips to the US, the first time to visit her daughter and the second time for Charlie's wedding.

**Herbert Hall.** Charlie's eldest brother was Herbert. He was born on 24th December 1897 and was the first of the family to be baptised in St. Margaret's Church. He was married to Dora, and they had two children called Ron and Jean. Ron was another member of the Hall family who became a regular at the early Laughing Gravy tent meetings.

Herbert (or Bert as he was known) lived in a back to back house in Vicarage Road.

Back to back houses were mainly for the working class. The houses were built literally back-to-back. You only had one entrance to the house, and you shared a backyard which contained the outside toilets and washhouse. After the slum clearances of the 1960's the only ones that remain in Birmingham are on the corner of Inge and Hurst Street. (They just happen to be right outside the Birmingham Hippodrome).

They have been restored and are now the property of the National Trust. So you can now visit them, and get a picture of what

*Charlie's brother Herbert Hall on his wedding day.*

it was like to live there. Bert was a 'joiner' by profession and served in the army in the First World War.

His daughter (Jean Cook) told me that Bert was: "On horses with guns," and that he came home unexpectedly to find his wife was seeing someone else. But we won't go into that!

Jean described her father as a 'joker' who had olive skin, and who worked outside a lot. According to Jean, Charlie asked Bert to go to America with him, but he did not want to leave his family.

Growing up Jean used to tell people that Charlie was her Uncle. She recalls that Stan and Ollie used to send them Christmas cards. They also sent her mom a green book with Laurel and Hardy on the front. It was signed by the duo and Jean gave it to her teacher, much to the disgust of her brother Ron.

Charlie (who Jean tells me used to cheat at cards when he used to play with Bert) may have sent the cards and book.

**Thomas Walter Hall** was born on 28th November 1902. (He was always known as Walter.) He was baptised at St. Margaret's Church on 17th December 1902. He was married to Katherine and they had two children called Pat and Bryan. Bryan describes his father as a quiet decent man, kind hearted, who never used to get angry or overreact. Like most people he would bet 'a few shillings' on The Derby or The Grand National, but in 1956 he placed a £5 bet on Birmingham City to win the FA Cup. This was quite a large bet for him. Unfortunately Birmingham lost in the final to Manchester City 1-3.

Walter was an extrusion die-maker and he served his apprentice at the Aston Chain & Stamp Hook Company in Erdington, Birmingham. Around 1964 he went to live in Australia for a while, but returned to the UK in 1972.

Bryan tells me that his family seemed to think it was 'no big deal' that Charlie was an actor. In fact they thought it was an odd thing to do. However they were all very fond of him, and Bryan never heard a bad word said about him.

Occasionally Bryan would hear his father say, "Our Charlie's on the telly."

Bryan's recollection of Charlie's fame is this:

*Charlie's brother Walter and his family on holiday.*

"Mother used to tell me he appeared with Laurel and Hardy, but I didn't think anything of it. It didn't occur to me to talk about it to anyone. At the time I just saw Laurel and Hardy as small time entertainers who filled in gaps during 'big films' at the cinema. I used to watch them and the Three Stooges, when we went to the cinema to see Flash Gordon. Would Uncle Charlie's connection have improved my street cred? I never used to mention them to anyone at school."

**Harry Hall** was born on March 25th 1905. He was married to Anne and they had two children called Joyce and June.

Like his father, Harry used to work for the Birmingham Corporation in the sewers. He was then promoted and managed to get Frank a job with him. He used to say that Frank had to work harder when he was around. Harry, like his brother Walter, was a Birmingham City supporter. Harry told his children about Charlie, but he didn't talk about him that much.

Joyce describes her father as a quiet and humble man, but he used to crack a lot of jokes. He served in the ARP during World War Two, and the family was sent away because they lived near the "GEC factory and railway, which was being bombed."

*Harry and Anne Hall with their daughters Joyce and June.*

**Arthur Hall** was born on 14th February 1908. He was baptised at St. Margaret's Church on 4th March 1908. As he was born on 14th February he was known as Arthur 'Valentine' Hall. Not much is known about Arthur. Joyce describes him as a 'wideboy', handsome and always smartly dressed. He lost touch with his family, and his whereabouts became unknown.

However very recently, new information has emerged about him. Dorothy Asprey (a relative) tells us that Arthur was a, "Lovely, lovely man. Always smiling and very smartly dressed."

*Arthur Hall standing outside his house in Wright Road, Alum Rock, Birmingham.*

His first wife was called Olive and they had three children. It seems he was a bit of a ladies' man, and a 'Clarke Gable lookalike'. He lived with his partner (Elsie) in Wright Road, Alum Rock, Birmingham, before emigrating to Australia in 1974. It was there that they were married.

He died of a heart attack on 22nd December 1981.

**Alfred Hall** was born on 28th November 1909. He was the last of Charlie's brothers to be baptised at St. Margaret's Church (on 29th December 1909).

He was married to Lilly, and they had four children: Bobby, Dennis, Jimmy and Hazel. They lived at 138 Tideswell Road, in the Great Barr area of Birmingham.

We know from Jimmy Hall that Alfred was a cable joiner (underground) for a company called Calendars Co. He also described him as a very quiet gentleman, who was always dressed in a suit and tie.

Like all Charlie's brothers, Alfred was proud of what Charlie had achieved. Although Jimmy never met Charlie's mother (Maria) he would often go to the Hall's house in Arley Road to visit Frank.

*At Jean Cook's wedding in 1954, Alfred is at the back on the right holding his daughter (Hazel).*

**Florence Matilda Hall** was born on 28th October 1902 and was baptised on 18th November 1900.

She left Birmingham on 30th December 1921 and set sail for Canada. She had secured a job working as a servant for Mrs. J Dean, Alice Street, Collingwood, Ontario.

*Left: Florence Hall. Right: Charlie with his sister Florence and his mother Maria.*

In July 1926 she made a return visit to Birmingham, to visit her family. She returned as Mrs. Florence Nellis. She stayed for 6 months before returning to the US. According to the records, her passage was paid for by her husband (John) and she gives her address in New York as Bedford Hills.

Joyce Perry thought Florence had plenty of money, as she would send herself and her sister (June) a lot of clothes.

"We used to have parcels come and it was great," said Joyce.

"We had lovely fitted dresses, and the other girls at school would always pass comments about them."

Joyce planned to go to the US to visit Florence or 'Auntie Floss' as she called her, but couldn't because of the war.

Charlie's mom had told her how great it was in the US. But the trip was not to be. However the war did not stop Florence sending over more parcels.

Florence and Charlie met up with Maria Hall for Charlie's wedding, which took place in 1935.

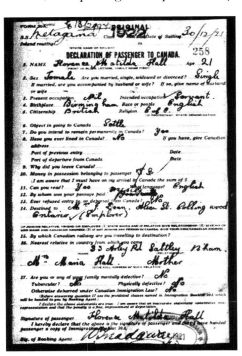

*Record of Florence Hall's passage to Canada*

**Ron Hall (Charlie's Nephew)**

In an interview given in 1994 Ron Hall recalled Charlie's visit. Ron, like various other members of the Hall family, seems to think that Charlie was suspended from the Hal Roach Studios.

Ron Hall was 64 when he gave this interview.

*"I was a little boy having an operation on my ear, and feeling very miserable. Suddenly this man walked down the ward, wearing a blazer, flannels, two-tone shoes and a colourful cravat. Quite a sight in the 1930's when everyone else was wearing drab clothes. It was Uncle Charlie who I'd never met before, home to visit his mother, my grandmother.*

*And he'd come to the hospital to visit ME – with the biggest box of chocolates you have ever seen.*

*That year he took me, his mother and a bunch of cousins up to Blackpool for a holiday. Even then, relaxing with his family, he couldn't resist performing.*

*All dressed up, he walked along the edge of a huge outdoor pool, pretending to be drunk. He wobbled up the diving board steps, several lifeguards in pursuit. It was just like a scene from one of his films.*

*Just before he was caught, he teetered on the edge of the board and fell off, creating a huge splash.*

*Ron Hall, John Ullah and Eileen Hall at one of Laughing Gravy's tent meetings.*

*The lifeguards panicked and fished him out, but it was all a joke. Us kids couldn't stop laughing, but he got a right telling off from our grandmother."*

Ron now gives his version on 'the sacking' of his Uncle Charlie.

*"Uncle Charlie was really good mates with Stan Laurel, and they were always going fishing.*

*Once in the middle of filming, Uncle Charlie, Laurel and Hardy, were given time off for a fishing weekend.*

*They must have been having a good time, because they didn't come back for five days. Hal Roach was furious and blamed Uncle Charlie, well he could hardly blame Laurel and Hardy, could he?*

*Uncle Charlie was sacked, virtually ending his career. He never worked with Laurel and Hardy again, and only had tiny bit parts in other films."*

Of course we know that Charlie did work with Laurel and Hardy again, although they would only make another two films at the Hal Roach Studios. Charlie, I'm pleased to say, had a small part in both of them.

Joyce Perry claims that all of the brothers got on really well and they were all really close. Having a famous Uncle never bothered her much, as people didn't believe her. But today she is proud of Charlie and what he achieved. Bryan is also proud of his uncle, and he is pleased that he is now getting recognition, after all these years.

*Chapter Fifteen*

# CHARLIE RETURNS TO THE U.S.

Back in the US in 1939, Charlie Hall found that he could still get work as an extra in various movies. And the movies and the people that he appeared with, were some of the biggest names in the film industry.

There was 'Five Came Back' (RKO) starring Lucille Ball in which Charlie played an airport worker.

'Man About Town' (Paramount Pictures) starring Jack Benny and Dorothy Lamour. In this film Charlie's part was a stage pageboy.

'Bachelor Mother' (RKO) starring Ginger Rogers and David Niven. Charlie has a part of a dance hall customer.

And finally one of the biggest films of the year 'The Hunchback of Notre Dame' with Charles Laughton and Maureen O'Hara. Charlie played the part of Mercury.

This was also the year that Charlie would make his last two films with Laurel and Hardy, 'A Chump at Oxford' (with a young Peter Cushing) and 'Saps at Sea'.

## A Chump at Oxford

The Hal Roach Studios put out a call for five young Englishmen to play students in his latest film 'A Chump at Oxford'. Facetiously adding 'Oxford students preferred'. Central Casting came back with Peter Cushing (who was working in the US at the time), Victor Kendall (a native of Moscow, but educated in Oxford), Gerald Rogers (a Londoner), Gerald Fielding (who was born in Darjeeling, India) and of course Charlie Hall (who was a very young 41 years old at the time).

In 'A Chump at Oxford', Laurel and Hardy help foil a bank robbery and the bank manager offers them an education as their reward. Not just any education, but the very best, and that means Oxford.

And so Laurel and Hardy arrive in Oxford to start their education.

They are at once the targets of a mischievous prank and they are led to a maze, which ensnares them. After many trials and tribulations they eventually make their way out, and are once again the targets for another prank.

This time they are led into a room, where four students are waiting for them. They have mortarboards on their heads and Charlie is wearing a false moustache. One of the students (who is pretending to be the Dean) introduces his fellow companions.

Charlie is introduced as Dr. Pigfoot, and the student next to him as his brother 'Trotter'. Laurel and Hardy are to be shown to "their quarters", which of course belongs to the Dean. They start singing, "For he's a jolly good fellow," and Charlie picks up their luggage and carries it into the Dean's room.

"And good luck. We don't think," the students say, and they doff their hats and leave the room.

A little later they check on how Stan and Ollie are coping in the Dean's room, but the Dean returns unexpectedly and they have to hide behind a screen.

The Dean enters his room to see Stan and Ollie have made themselves completely at home and they are smoking his cigars and drinking his liquor (or nightcap, as Stan calls it).

The Dean is furious but Stan and Ollie think it is another prank, and they try to throw the Dean out. At this point we see the screen moving towards the door (carried by the students) but they are knocked over by someone entering the room.

All is revealed as Stan and Ollie explain how they came to be in his room. The students are furious and call them "Snitches," and walk out.

Apparently there is one thing they won't tolerate in Oxford, and that's snitching!

The scene moves on to lines of students (one of which is Charlie), who have linked hands and are singing, "Fee, Fi, Fo, Fum, we want the blood of an American."

Stan and Ollie look out of the window to see what all the commotion is about. "We'll chew them up like chewing gum," the song continues, and they point to Stan and Ollie.

Their aim is to take the breeches off the boys and throw them out of the window onto a blanket. They enter the room, but Stan who has bumped his head has now reverted to Lord Paddington.

"What is the meaning of this vulgar intrusion?" Stan says, in a very upper class accent.

Charlie replies, "You know what we mean. We're going to take off your breeches and run you out of Oxford."

Stan, is offended by this and replies, "What. Take off my breeches? In the presence of Meredith."

"Yes, you little snitcher," says Charlie.

"Repeat that remark again?" Stan replies.

"Dirty snitcher," the students shout.

Stan wiggles his ears and throws the students out of the window one by one. Many consider this film as Laurel and Hardy's last great adventure, but there was still 'Saps at Sea' to come.

### Saps at Sea

Fittingly, Charlie Hall's last appearance in a Laurel and Hardy film, would also be Stan and Ollie's last film at the Hal Roach Studios. It was called 'Saps at Sea'. Charlie's role in this film is very brief.

Ollie comes down a flight of stairs and enters the lobby. Charlie is behind the desk.

"Where is the basement?" Ollie asks Charlie.

"Downstairs," Charlie replies.

"Thank you."

"You're welcome."

*Charlie plays a desk clerk in his last Laurel and Hardy film 'Saps at Sea'.*

At this point Charlie does a double take, as he realises what he has just said. A few minutes later and this time Stan comes down the stairs (carrying a mattress).

"Which way to the alley."

"Out on the street," says Charlie.

"Thanks very much."

Again Charlie looks a little startled. Stan puts the mattress on the back of a car for Ollie to fall on (as he is now hanging out of a window). But he reverses the car by mistake, and it crashes into the lobby.

Stan says to Charlie, "Excuse me, I was just coming," and he immediately drives back out.

Charlie Hall's last Laurel and Hardy film ends with Oliver Hardy saying to Stan Laurel, "Here's another nice mess you've gotten me into!"

Thirteen years after his first appearance with Laurel and Hardy, Charlie Hall and his pals went their separate ways. Stan and Ollie would soon be off to 20th Century Fox in a move they hoped would give them even greater control of the films they were making. This of course was not to be, and there was no room for Charlie in the remainder of their films.

*Chapter Sixteen*

# LIFE WITHOUT STAN AND OLLIE

In 1940 Charlie was again appearing with Edgar Kennedy, in Edgar's 'Average Man' series, and he also appeared with Abbott and Costello in their film 'One Night in the Tropics'.

During the years 1941–1950 Charlie was still popping up in various movies. In the 1942 film 'The Big Street' which stars Henry Fonda and Lucille Ball, Charlie has a small scene with Henry Fonda.

As they are waiting for a table of guests to leave, Charlie (who plays the waiter) says to Henry Fonda, "It's about time," and looks at his watch.

"Four o'clock and I've got a suspicious wife."

Trying hard not to look at the camera Charlie walks off.

In 1943 Charlie appeared in 'Shot in the Escape' which starred his old friend from the Hal Roach Studios, Billy Gilbert. Billy Gilbert was the voice of Sneezy in Snow White and the Seven Dwarfs. But to all Laurel and Hardy fans he was Professor Theodore von Schwarzenhoffen M.D. A.D. D.D.S. F.L.D. F.F.F. & F. in 'The Music Box'.

'Shot in the Escape' is about a hen pecked husband who is allowed out by his wife to go to the pictures with his friend (Cliff Nazarro). On the way Billy offers to carry a woman (Barbara Slater) across a muddy street. Both he and Cliff end up getting soaked and the woman asks them back to her apartment, to dry their clothes.

The woman's husband (Charlie Hall) turns up just as Cliff says to Charlie's wife, "Hey, toots. Hurry up with my pants and things, we gotta get out of here."

Charlie thinks something is going on, and he is still eavesdropping when Billy notices Charlie's photograph and says, "I wonder who that sour kisser is?"

They move over to a picture of a dog and this time Billy says, "Get a load of the ears on this guy."

Charlie thinks he is talking about him, and he bursts in from behind the door. "This has gone far enough" he snaps.

They realise that Charlie is the woman's husband, and Billy tries to explain their predicament. He picks up Charlie to show him how he "picked

*Charlie poses for the camera.*

up his wife". As he is doing so, Charlie produces a gun. Billy drops Charlie, and both he and his friend make their way onto the fire escape. Charlie opens a window and shoots at them. Both are hit in the backside by ricocheting bullets. Charlie shouts after them,

"There you are you home wreckers. Trying to steal my wife."

As Billy and Cliff make their way down the fire escape, their wives just happen to be passing. They see what is happening and one of them comments, "I'm glad our husbands don't get up to anything like that."

When they realise it is their husbands, they chase after them, but end up falling in a big hole in the road. End of film.

Charlie can also be seen in 'The Lodger' (1944) with George Sanders, 'Dressed to Kill' (aka UK Sherlock Homes and the Secret Code 1946) with Basil Rathbone and Nigel Bruce. And in 1948 Charlie appeared in his last 'Average Man' series as a painter in the film 'Home Canning'. Edgar Kennedy would only make one more film in this series called 'Contest Crazy'. Edgar Kennedy passed away just a few weeks later.

In 1950 Charlie made an appearance in another famous film called 'The Milkman', starring Donald O'Connor and Jimmy Durante.

Of course when he wasn't working in films, Charlie would turn his hand to making props. He was a very skilful carpenter, and this occupation was proving to be very useful indeed.

In 1952 Charlie Hall appeared in the film 'Limelight'. His part was only to last a few seconds, as a newspaper seller on a street. "News, Extra" Charlie shouts.

However the person he shouts it to, idly walks past. That person, was none other than Charlie Chaplin.

*Chapter Seventeen*

# CHARLIE APPEARS ON T.V.

Charlie Hall had gone from silent movies to the talkies and now we can find him on T.V.

In 1953 he appeared with Abbott and Costello in an episode of one of their T.V. series. He is listed in the cast as Charles Hall.

In the episode that includes Charlie, Abbott and Costello act as decoys to get two girls out of a house. The reason for this is that the girls want to meet two hoodlums their father would not approve of.

The girl's father is crazy about birds, and he wants to put an aerial on the roof (in the shape of a birdcage) so he can watch a programme about birds later on in the day. Abbot and Costello offer to put the aerial on the roof and it's here that they meet Charlie.

Charlie is tarmacking the roof, and doesn't see Abbott and Costello behind him. Lou Costello falls, and the aerial shaped birdcage goes over Charlie's head.

Charlie falls unconvincingly into the tarmac. He picks himself up and says, "Hey, what are you guys doing up here with that bird cage?"

Bud duly explains and Charlie replies, "Well keep out of my way while I work. Now be careful where you walk, there's some weak spots in this roof."

"Dangerous eh," replies Bud.

"Yep," says Charlie.

"Well thanks for the tip. My name is Bud Abbott," and they shake hands. For a few seconds their hands stick together, as Charlie has tar on his.

Abbott and Costello begin to put up the aerial, as Charlie continues working just in front of them. Lou falls over again and gets stuck in the tarmac. Bud goes behind him to help him up, but cannot manage it. Charlie enters and offers to help.

"Wait a minute. I'll help you," he says. He goes behind Bud, and starts pulling. This results in Charlie landing on his back with Bud Abbott on top of him.

Bud explains that it was an accident. "One more accident, and I'm gonna get mad," says Charlie, as he pushes Bud off him.

Because Abbott and Costello haven't brought the girls out of the house, the two hoodlums think they have been double-crossed. They go onto the roof and a fight breaks out. Charlie gets caught in the middle.

"What's going on?" he says, and gets a brush full of tar in his face, which causes him to fall over. In the melee, Lou Costello falls through the roof.

"He hit the roof and disappeared," one of the hoodlums says.

"He's probably down in the cellar," replies Charlie with a blackened face.

Lou Costello's fall has seen him land onto a bed and he gets covered in feathers. He staggers into the living room. The girl's father thinks he is some kind of rare bird and he takes his gun to shoot it, but he is stopped. End of show.

By the mid fifties Charlie's health was beginning to deteriorate, possibly due to his excessive drinking. He does crop up in the 1955 Warner Bros. Film 'Illegal', which starred Edward G. Robinson. And in the following year we have Charlie Hall's last known film called 'So you want to play the Piano' with George O'Hanlon.

Charlie plays the role of a piano mover called Clyde.

The joke is that the two piano movers can play the piano better than Joe McDoakes (George O'Hanlon) who's bought the piano to impress his wife.

1956 also saw Charlie make an appearance in the popular TV series 'Cheyenne' starring Clint Walker. This series was made by Warner Bros., and we know that Charlie was working there as a prop maker at this time. The episode Charlie appeared in is called 'Quicksand', and it also co-starred Dennis Hopper (as the Utah Kid).

Charlie plays the role of Kevin, a passenger on a stagecoach, which overturns as it is fleeing from Comanche Indians. All the occupants manage to get out of the overturned stagecoach and get to an abandoned shack. The Indians start shooting, and Charlie, Clint and the others shoot back. Charlie then looks up to Clint Walker and says (in a cockney accent) "They're gawn".

It appears that they may be held up for some time, and this annoys Dennis Hopper, who draws a gun on Clint Walker. Clint tells him to put the gun away, which prompts Charlie to point his rifle at Dennis's head and say, "You heard what he said". Dennis puts the gun away (later on in the episode Cheyenne kills Dennis Hopper, The Utah Kid, in a gunfight).

However the siege goes on and Charlie has an idea. He turns to Clint Walker and suggests someone should ride for help. Clint states the odds are 100-1 against anyone making it. Undeterred Charlie gets out a pack of cards, and offers them around (High card goes for help). As you might have guessed it's Charlie who draws the high card and he rides for help.

However the Indians capture him, and they tie him to a tree. Of course Cheyenne eventually rescues him, and completes a challenge in quicksand against a Comanche Indian, to save everyone else.

Also in this year, Charlie managed to get himself a small part in the Alfred Hitchcock TV series called 'Alfred Hitchcock Presents'. The episode Charlie appears in is called 'Safe Conduct'. It was aired on 19th February 1956, and Charlie's part was a 'man with a pool cue'.

## Chapter 18

# CHARLIE'S LATER YEARS

In 1957 Charlie and Wilda were still living at 5622 Willow Crest Avenue, North Hollywood. And it was here that once again Charlie writes to his old friend George Stevens for help. We believe the letter was sent early December 1957 (letter nine).

The letter is self-explanatory, as is George Steven's reply to Charlie dated 6th December 1957 (letter ten).

We can see the reply from the Screen Directors Guild to George Stevens, rejecting Charlie's application due to the amount of unemployment amongst people who already hold cards (letter eleven). It seems that not even George Stevens could help Charlie out this time.

*Charlie's house in Willow Crest Avenue, North Hollywood, USA. This photograph was taken in 2006.*

Charles Hall,
5622 Willowcrest Ave,
North Hollywood,
Phone PO 30700.

"Hi George"
"I saw yer throw the bannana, picking on the little feller, why for two pins", I,d", well thats enough of that!

George the reason I am writing you, I applied yesterday for a membership card as second assistant director at the Screen Directors Guild. They told me I should contact Directors that I had worked with in the past years for reference. You and Leo, George were the first ones I thought of, Leo Mc Carey that is. Would it be too much

*Letter nine.*

152

George, to ask you to put in a good word for me. I know you are a very busy person on preparation of your next picture, but if you can spare the time I sure will appreciate it.

Good luck George, I hope you have another Acadamy winner

Thanks

Charlie

*Letter nine contin…*

December 6, 1957

Dear Charlie --

Glad to get your letter.   It was good to hear from you.

I am getting in touch with the Directors Guild to see
if there is anything I can do to be helpful in the matter
that you speak about.    I will let you know.

Best of luck, Charlie, and all good wishes.

Cordially,

George Stevens

Charles Hall
5622 Willowcrest Avenue
North Hollywood

*Letter ten.*

Mr Stevens —

Regarding Charlie Hall's application to the SDG for an assistant director's card .... there just isn't a chance at this time because of all the un-employment of fellows who already hold cards.

Would do no harm, I am told, if you would care to write a letter to the Guild saying something to the effect that you would appreciate it if his application could be given consideration when the situation changes and new members are being admitted.

L.

XXXXX

12/11/57

*Letter eleven.*

The following day George writes to Charlie to tell him the news (letter twelve). Charlie duly replies, thanking George for his help, (letter thirteen). Charlie Hall's next letter to George Stevens is written from the St. Joseph's Hospital, Burbank, California. We don't know the date, but it is around 1957. Charlie's in hospital for an operation (letter fourteen).

Charlie has come through the operation, and is now back home at Willow Crest Avenue (letter fifteen). He writes a moving letter to George Stevens, thanking him for sending him a gift, and for just being a good friend.

Charlie's next letter to George Stevens is an interesting one (letter sixteen). Charlie obviously has time on his hands and has come up with an idea for a comedy series. We don't know if George Stevens took up Charlie's suggestion, but it seems unlikely.

In June 1958 Charlie Hall appeared on a very famous US quiz show hosted by Groucho Marx. The show was called 'You Bet Your Life'. His first appearance was on the 16th June (on radio) and his second on the 19th June on TV.

It is believed that once again Charlie took on the role of a cockney character, when answering questions from Groucho.

Other guests included Anna Mae Devereux and Joseph Cossman, Helen Gerson, Max de Sousa and Tony Fernandez.

Groucho Marx interviews the contestants and if they mentioned the 'secret word' they would win $100. The secret word when Charlie was on the show was 'walk'.

If the secret word was mentioned during the interview a card (with the word on it) suspended from a duck would drop down from above. It was fitting that Charlie was on the show on the 16th June, as this was the date of Stan Laurel's birthday.

On December 13th 1958 Charlie once again writes to George Stevens asking him for help. Charlie wants to be reinstated at Central Casting. Could George Stevens use his influence to achieve this? (letter seventeen).

Although we only have George Steven's letter to the Central Casting Corporation, dated 22nd October 1959, it once again shows how highly he regards Charlie (letter eighteen).

However just a few months after this letter on Monday 7th December, Charlie Hall passed away at his home in Willow Crest Avenue. He was 60 years old. His wife Wilda was with him when he died.

He was buried on 10th December 1959 at the Forest Lawn Cemetery, Glendale, USA.

December 12, 1957


Dear Charlie –

I have talked with the Screen Directors Guild,
Assistants Branch, about your application for
an assistant director's card and have discovered
there just isn't a chance at this time because
of the unemployment of many who already
hold cards.

I am sorry I can't help you but I would suggest
that you try again if and when there is a pick-
up in business in the industry.

Best as always.




Charles Hall
5622 Willowcrest Ave.
North Hollywood

*Letter twelve.*

Charlie Hall

Thanks George
for everything.
better luck next time.
If you need a good bloke
for an assistant props, I have
a 44 Local card.
I hope the kid makes
good tonight on his show "People"
trusting a little of your ability
rubbed on him
Charlie

*Letter thirteen.*

*Printed Christmas card sent by Charlie and his wife.*

**Saint Joseph Hospital**
BURBANK, CALIFORNIA

Hi George
I bet you are
all exited with your
coming opening of your
picture! I wish you the
best George. I'm in
for a retake, operate at
9.30 A.M. Thursday.
I'll be a seeing you
Best Alway's
Charlie

*Letter fourteen.*

Saint Joseph Hospital
BURBANK, CALIFORNIA

Charlie Hall,
5622 Willowcrest Ave,
North Hollywood,
Po 30700.

Hi George
                  well its good to be
back home.        George I
want to thank you from the
bottom of my heart for your
kindness and thougthfulness. Its
nice George to have someone
call you when you're flat on
your back and one feels like he
does not have a friend in the
world, It does one so much
good to hear a friends vioce, it
helps one to keep his pecker up.
        I also want to thank you for
the Ayalea plant, it is just

*Letter fifteen.*

Saint Joseph Hospital
BURBANK, CALIFORNIA

simply goregeous. Tell me how
did you know growing Ayaleas
is my hobby, not only that, but
you sent me one that I do not
have, believe me I can't wait
to plant it.          Well George
I'll let you go, and again I thank
you for your kindness, thats what
makes you a thoroughbred George,
thats more than I can say for
some of my fair weather friends
such as the great D-Arcy whom
I fed for weeks before he got
his break with Jack Webb, but
I still wish the guy luck
  "Well Cheerio,
        I saw you throw the bannane
Why for two pins"

*Letter fifteen contin…*

I'll be seeing you someday
and I'll thank you in person
Bye now
Best Always
Charlie

*Letter fifteen contin…*

Charlie Hall.
5622 Willowcrest Ave,
North Hollywood,'
Po 30700

Hi George
yes, I'm still alive and kicking.
George, I heard through the grape-
-vine that you are contemplating going
in to T.V.  I have an idea for a
comedey series, which I think you
might be interested.  Would like
to take a few minuetes of your time some
-day to say hello.  I know George you
are a very busy person, so if you do
not have the time to spare, I wish you
the best always.  Thanks George,
the Ayealeas are doing terriffic
Charlie

*Letter sixteen.*

Charles Hall,
5622 Willowcrest Ave,
North Hollywood,
Dec-13ᵗʰ 58

phone - Poplar 30700

Hi George just to let you know I am
still living. "What did you say"?
"Thats too bad." I hope you've got an
Oscar winning picture. George Here I
am asking another favor, as a Producer
all I ask of you is to get me reinstated at
Central Casting. Hal Roach gave me a
letter to them but it did no good; for the
simple reason the Studio does not hire
through Central Casting. Mr Frank
Freeman is President and Mr Maury Weiner
Vice President of Central Casting. If you
can get me reinstated George I sure will
appreciate it Thanks and a Merry Xmas
Charlie

*Letter seventeen.*

October 22, 1959

Mr Art Bronson
Central Casting Corporation
5504 Hollywood Boulevard
Hollywood 28

Dear Mr Bronson:

I know very well that you continually face a problem of having a great many more people available than the demand calls for. Despite this knowledge I want to make a plea to you on behalf of Charlie Hall in the hope that it would be possible for him to be reinstated in an active position on your rolls after a very long period of absence.

Mr Hall — I believe you know him — has had a long career in the acting phase of our industry, despite an absence from it in recent years. He was first an extra with Hal Roach, Sennett and others, starting about 1924 and continuing for a number of years, when he developed into an able comedian and played bits, then parts, and had some featured experience for quite a long period of time, holding a card in the Screen Actors Guild. Later, as I recollect, he was active in the Screen Extras Guild and dropped out in 1942. He worked with me and many of my associates in a great number of pictures. We thought highly of him and he was a credit to the organizations to which he belonged.

He is very desirous of being reinstated in the Screen Extras Guild. I think it would be a fine thing if you could find this reinstatement to be possible; and I would personally do much to recommend him for work among the people I know who could use him in the industry.

Very sincerely yours,

George Stevens

Charlie Hall
5622 Willowcrest Avenue
North Hollywood
telephone: POplar 3-0700

*Letter eighteen.*

*Flowers left by Charlie's home tent (Laughing Gravy) at his resting place.*

Interestingly on his death certificate, under the name and birthplace of his father, it reads 'Unknown Hall', England. And under the name and birthplace of his mother it simply reads 'Maria Unknown England'.

His last occupation is listed as 'Prop Maker', at the Warner Bros. Studios. His wife Wilda lists her present or last occupation as 'Housewife'.

Wilda 'Foxie' Hall died on 21st October 1966, at the Motion Picture Hospital. She is buried alongside Charlie in the Forest Lawn, Cemetery.

Charlie's marker reads 'Beloved Husband' and Wilda's reads 'Auntie'.

*Chapter Nineteen*

# CHARLIE HALL,
# GONE BUT NOT FORGOTTEN

In late 1999 I was on my way to my local Post Office, when I noticed that the old Bingo Hall in Barnabas Road, Erdington, Birmingham was being converted into a pub. The company that was converting the hall into a pub was called J.D.Wetherspoon. They have many outlets throughout the UK, and they like their pub names to have a local connection.

I wrote to them and asked if they had a name for the new pub in Barnabas Road, and I offered my own suggestion, which was of course 'The Charlie Hall'. I included a photograph of Charlie with Laurel and Hardy, to make my point.

A few days later I had a phone call from J.D.Wetherspoons. They told me that they already had a name for the pub and it was to be called 'The Thomas Holte'. However they were very intrigued in the name Charlie Hall.

*Members of The Laughing Gravy tent of Birmingham outside the Charlie Hall pub.*

*Charlie's great nieces and nephew – Jane, Steve, Jill and Elizabeth – at The Charlie Hall pub on the opening night.*

We had a brief conversation about Charlie (in which I gave them a few details and facts about him) and I was told to expect a call in the next few days. Apparently plans for 'The Thomas Holte' were well underway, but I was told they thought 'The Charlie Hall' had a nice ring to it.

To my absolute delight J.D. Wetherspoon had a change of heart and the new pub was indeed to be called 'The Charlie Hall'. Could we supply as many photographs as possible to hang in the pub? We duly obliged, and on 24th May 2000, 'The Charlie Hall' was opened.

The 'Charlie Hall' is a huge pub, and when we arrived on the opening night, it was absolutely packed. To our complete surprise we found that some of Charlie's relatives had come along to celebrate the opening of the pub in his name.

One or two 'Sons of the Dessert' from up and down the country also joined us, and it's fair to say many toasts were made to Charlie that night. As I live only a few minutes walk away, it's nice to say that my local pub is called 'The Charlie Hall'.

In 2009 Leigh Road School celebrated its Centenary. We were invited along (we being Mandy Finney, Kevin Pullinger and myself) to join in the celebrations. We set up a film show of Laurel and Hardy movies featuring Charlie Hall, and afterwards I gave a brief talk on Charlie's life.

Then current pupils marked the school's 100 year history, with various dances. Each year group performed a dance from a different decade. The Charleston for the twenties, and Rock n' Roll for the fifties. Then to our delight, to represent the thirties, two pupils recreated the dance from the Laurel and Hardy film 'Way Out West'.

It was a wonderful feeling to walk in the corridors, and sit in the classrooms, as Charlie did all those years ago.

Then on Saturday 6th June 2010, we decided to honour Charlie with a Laurel & Hardy 'Hall Day' in Birmingham. Jean Cook was our special guest and she raised a glass to "Uncle Charlie", to tremendous cheers.

*Jean Cook.*

*Local artist Colin Whittock's view of the first 'Hall Day' held in Birmingham in 2010.*

Charlie Hall the little man from Ward End, Birmingham, England must have had an incredible life. He lived through two world wars, and was part of the wonderful silent comedy world, that developed into talkies and then onto T.V.

He worked with some of the greatest silent comedians of all times, and he was lucky enough to appear in some of the greatest movies of all time. Charlie, as we have seen, would often become the 'Little Menace', but to his family he was a very kind, decent man. Highly thought of, and very fondly remembered.

In his wildest dreams he could not have imagined what lay in store for him, as he set sail to the US all those years ago. He may never be a household name, but here in his home city of Birmingham, he will never be forgotten.

*Chapter Twenty*

# THE SONS OF THE DESERT: THE WORLDWIDE LAUREL AND HARDY APPRECIATION SOCIETY

In November 1953 a young American graduate student (John McCabe) was on his way to the Birmingham Library to do some research. He was studying at the Shakespeare Institute in Stratford-upon-Avon, but his studies frequently took him into Birmingham. His route to the library took him past the Birmingham Hippodrome, where he noticed a poster, which read Laurel and Hardy 'Here in Person' appearing in 'Birds of a Feather'.

John McCabe claimed that he knew nearly all the films Laurel and Hardy made, but did not know anything about 'Birds of a Feather'. ('Birds of a Feather' was in fact a sketch written by Stan Laurel specifically for this tour).

He went to see the show, and afterwards went backstage to meet his heroes. In fact John McCabe went backstage most of the nights that Laurel and Hardy were in Birmingham. It was the start of a wonderful friendship, which would eventually lead to the formation of an organisation, which now has a worldwide following. That organisation is called the Sons of the Desert.

'Sons of the Desert' is a 1933 Laurel and Hardy film where Ollie feigns illness to attend a convention in Chicago (his wife won't let him go!) and he takes Stan with him.

In the film, Laurel and Hardy both wore a Fez to go to the convention. And nearly all Sons of the Desert own a Fez. In 1978 Laurel and Hardy fans worldwide gathered, fittingly in Chicago, for the first International Convention of the Sons of the Desert. Amongst the celebrities who attended were Anita Garvin and Della Lind.

An International convention takes place every two years, and I'm proud to say that the Laughing Gravy tent of Birmingham won the right to stage the 1998 International Convention.

*Sons of the Desert.*

A UK convention is held every year and the first one was also held in 1978. Bill Cubin and the Berth Marks tent of Ulverston hosted it. In 1993 the European convention was launched. All the conventions still run to this day. Each branch (or tent as we call it) of the Sons of the Desert takes their name from a Laurel and Hardy film.

In 1993 I decided to start a tent here in Birmingham. As luck would have it, the two people who answered my call for help were Barrie Finney and Steve Smith. Barrie was a graphic designer by trade, and he would design our

*1998 International convention logo. Designed by Barrie Finney.*

magnificent tent logo and he also hand made our tent banner. His wonderful drawings are still used today by many tents, and his work is well respected by all. Sadly Barrie passed away in 2002. He is greatly missed by all Sons of the Desert.

When I first met Steve Smith he worked for Central TV. He owned a projector and set about buying 16mm prints of Laurel & Hardy films, to show at our meetings.

Our first meeting was appropriately held on Thursday 1st April 1993 (April Fools Day), and we still meet on the first Thursday of every month. We could only have one name – Laughing Gravy in honour of Charlie Hall.

Stan Laurel helped out with the Sons' Constitution, and he insisted that nothing is taken too seriously, and the society has a "half-assed dignity" about it. Below is the constitution, as Stan wanted it.

*Laughing Gravy's Tent logo. Also designed by Barrie Finney.*

**Article I**

The Sons of the Desert is an organisation with scholarly overtones and heavily social undertones devoted to the loving study of the persons and films of Stan Laurel and Oliver Hardy.

**Article II**

The founding members are Orson Bean, Al Kilgore, John McCabe, Chuck McCann and John Municino.

**Article III**

The Sons of the Desert shall have the following officers and board members who will be elected at an annual meeting:

Grand Sheik

Vice – Sheik (Sheik in charge of vice)

Sub – Vice Vizier (Sheik Treasurer, and in charge of sub-vice)

Grand Vizier (Corresponding Secretary)

Board Members-at-large (This number should not exceed 812)

**Article IV**

All officers and board members-at-large shall sit at an exalted place at the annual banquet.

**Article V**

The officers and board members-at-large shall have absolutely no authority whatsoever.

**Article VI**

Despite his absolute lack of authority, the Grand Sheik or his deputy shall act as chairman at all meetings and will follow the standard parliamentary procedure in conducting same. At the meetings, it is hoped that the innate dignity, sensitivity, and good taste of the members assembled will permit activities to be conducted with a lively sense of deportment and good order.

**Article VII**

Article VI is ridiculous.

**Article VIII**

The annual meeting shall be conducted in the following sequence:

1  Cocktails
2  Business meeting and cocktails
3  Dinner (with cocktails)
4  After-dinner speeches and cocktails
5  Cocktails
6  Coffee and Cocktails
7  Showing of Laurel and Hardy films
8  After film critique and cocktails
9  After-after-film critique and cocktails
10 Stan has suggested this period. In his words "All members are requested to park their camels and hire a taxi; then return for "One for the desert"!

**Article IX**
Section '4' above shall consist in part of the following toasts:
"To Stan"
"To Babe"
"To Fin"
"To Mae Busch and Charlie Hall – who are eternally ever-popular".

**Article X**
Section '8' above shall include the reading of scholarly papers on Laurel and Hardy. Any member going over an 8 1/2 minute time limit will have his cocktails limited to fourteen.

**Article XI**
Hopefully, and seriously, the Sons of the Desert, in the strong desire to perpetuate the spirit and genius of Laurel and Hardy, will conduct activities ultimately and always devoted to the preservation of their films and the encouragement of their showing everywhere.

**Article XII**
There shall be member societies in other cities called "Tents", each of which shall derive its name from one of the films.

**Article XIII**
Stan has suggested that members might wear a fez or blazer with an appropriate motto. He says, "I hope that the motto can be blue and grey, showing two derbies with these words superimposed: 'Two minds without a single thought'."

I have been a member of the Sons of the Desert for over twenty years and have attended many conventions. Recently after many years of fundraising, we presented Stan's hometown of Ulverston with a magnificent bronze statue of Stan and Ollie. On the back of the statue is 'poor little Laughing Gravy' pulling at Ollie's trousers.

*Ken Dodd at the statue unveiling.*

On a beautiful sunny afternoon in April 2009, Ken Dodd unveiled the statue to thunderous applause. Eric Woods represented our organisation, and Graham Ibbeson (who sculpted the statue) was also there. The statue takes pride of place in the County Square, in front of the Coronation Hall. It is overlooked by the balcony where Stan and Ollie once stood.

There are many 'tents' of the Sons of the Desert. At one such meeting, Tony Hawes (who was married to Stan Laurel's daughter Lois) raised his glass in a toast to Charlie and said,

"As a straight man, a foil or a dupe
Charlie Hall was the best in his group
So our glasses we raise
As upwards we gaze
To that house up there on the stoop".

And at this very minute someone somewhere may well be raising a glass to Birmingham's very own Charlie Hall.

\*   \*   \*   \*   \*

# ACKNOWLEDGEMENTS

I would like to thank the following people who have helped me with this book: Marshall Korby, Ray Andrew, Leo Brooks, Yair Solan, Josie Jukes, Dean McKeown, Bryan Hall, Jean Cook, Joyce Perry, Iris Summers, Ron Hall, Simon Hall, Jimmy Hall, Dorothy Aspey, Irv Hyatt, Tony Bagley, Tony Hillman, Colin Whittock, Willie McIntrye, Marion Grave, Dave Crump, David Millin, The Weekly News, and The Sunday Mercury.

Special mention must go to the following:

**Dave Wyatt**
For helping me with the very detailed Charlie Hall filmography, and for proof reading my book. Dave also provided some crucial information about Charlie, which helped me to tie up quite a few loose ends. His helpful advice, and knowledge of movies in general, means I can contact him anytime and find answers to my questions. He was recently involved in a horrific house fire, but to everyone's relief, he has made a remarkable recovery. Thanks for everything Dave.

**Bill Cassara**
Bill Cassara is the main reason for me writing this book. It was while reading his own book on another of Laurel and Hardy's co-stars, Edgar Kennedy (Master of the Slow Burn) that I decided to write this book about Charlie. Whenever I need a bit of advice, Bill is someone I can always rely on. He even paid a $2 invoice for some research material for me! Bill lives in Monterey, USA, and we have been friends since 1996. He is hoping that one day he will be able to visit the UK. When he does, he has promised to head for Birmingham, where we can have a pint or two in the Charlie Hall pub. I'll pay. Cheers Bill!

**Audrey Ryan**
Audrey Ryan is one of our Laughing Gravy tent members. She first came to one of our meetings in June 2007. Audrey works at Leigh Road School, and is a member of the Ward End Historical Society. Her enthusiasm and knowledge of local history is second to none. She is a wonderful character. It's always great fun to be in her company, and we have shared many laughs

together. I owe Audrey so much, especially for finding Charlie's family records, and for taking the time to show me around the workings of the Birmingham Library.

## Roger Robinson

Roger started the Saps at Sea tent of Southend in 1998. The Saps at Sea, and our own Laughing Gravy tent are 'twinned', and we have held many special events between us over the years. Roger's foreword to my book is typical of his sense of humour and clever play on words. He represents the very best of the Sons of the Desert, and I'm proud to say he is a very good friend of mine.

## Irv Hyatt

Irv Hyatt has sent me numerous DVD's to watch regarding Charlie Hall. For this, I am very grateful, as I hadn't seen most of these films before. He is about to have his own book published tentatively titled "Two for the Road: Laurel and Hardy on Tour". This will be a must for all Laurel and Hardy fans.

## Mandy Finney

Mandy and I have been together for over 15 years. This book could not have been written without her. Mandy constantly checks my work, and corrects my grammar. Otherwise this is my book what I wrote. As you can see she hasn't checked this section. Thanks Mand for all your help.

*For more information about Laughing Gravy and the Laurel & Hardy Appreciation Society check the following websites:* **www.laughinggravytent.co.uk**, **www.bowlerdessert.co.uk**.

# CHARLIE HALL FILMOGRAPHY

Charlie Hall can be very difficult to spot in certain films. He may only be in a scene for a few seconds. So compiling this filmography has been very challenging. Listed below are the films Charlie is known to have appeared in, (including some films where his part was cut).

As he mainly worked as an extra, there may be more appearances we are yet to discover. I'm sure I will still be getting calls and e-mails along the line of, "I think have just spotted Charlie in ……."

But until then, here is Charlie Hall's Filmography as we know it.

Note – the films are set out as follows: **TITLE** Studio, Distributor, number of reels, leading actors and series, date and month of release, (Charlie's role).

## 1923

**MOTHER'S JOY** Hal Roach. Pathe. 2 Reels. Stan Laurel series. 23/12 (houseguest)

## 1924

**SMITHY** Hal Roach. Pathe. 2 Reels. Stan Laurel 20/1 (one of building workers)
**COWBOY SHEIK** Hal Roach. 2 Reels. Will Rogers 3/2 (man at dance)
**POSTAGE DUE** Hal Roach. Pathe. 2 Reels. Stan Laurel 17/2 (customer)
**ZEB VS. PAPRIKA** Hal Roach. Pathe. 2 Reels. Stan Laurel. 16/3 (spectator)
**BIG MOMENTS FROM LITTLE PICTURES** Hal Roach. Pathe. 2 Reels. Will Rogers series. 30/3 (Chaplin type cop & one of Robin Hood's men)
**NEAR DUBLIN** Hal Roach. Pathe. 2 Reels. Stan Laurel 11/5 (villager in hayloft)
**GOING TO CONGRESS** Hal Roach. Pathe. 2 Reels. Will Rogers. 25/5 (farm boy in crowd)
**A TEN MINUTE EGG** Hal Roach. Pathe. 1 Reel. Charley Chase series. 20/7 (bellhop)
**THE BATTLING ORIOLES** Hal Roach. Pathe. 6 Reels. Glenn Tryon series 26/10 (baseball player)

# 1925

**THE GOLD RUSH** Charles Chaplin Productions. United Artists. 9 Reels. Charlie Chaplin 16/8 (Charlie claimed to have appeared in the climactic shipboard scene, but no shots of him can be found in current prints)

**BAD BOY** Hal Roach Pathe. ?? Reels. Charley Chase 12/4 (dance hall tough guy)

**BIG RED RIDING HOOD** Hal Roach. Pathe. 1 Reel. Charley Chase 26/4 (book thief)

**ISN'T LIFE TERRIBLE** Hal Roach. Pathe. 2 Reels. Charley Chase. 5/7 (steward who drops plates)

**MADAME SANS JANE** Hal Roach. Pathe. 2 Reels. Glenn Tryon 9/8

**UNFRIENDLY ENEMIES** Hal Roach. Pathe. 1 Reel. James Finlayson series. 13/9 (first soldier over the top)

# 1926

**GOOD CHEER** Hal Roach. Pathe. 2 Reels. Our Gang series 10/1 (motorist & pedestrian)

**BURIED TREASURE** Hal Roach. Pathe. 2 Reels. Our Gang 14/2 (man in gorilla suit)

**MONKEY BUSINESS** Hal Roach. Pathe. 2 Reels. Our Gang 21/3 (balloon vendor)

**UKULELE SHEIKS** Hal Roach. Pathe. 2 Reels. Glenn Tryon. 11/4 (explorer)

**BABY CLOTHES** Hal Roach Pathe. 2 Reels. Our Gang. 25/4 (bellboy)

**THUNDERING FLEAS** Hal Roach. Pathe. 2 Reels. Our Gang 4/7 (musician)

**MIGHTY LIKE A MOOSE** Hal Roach. Pathe. 2 Reels. Charley Chase 18/7 (shoeshine boy)

**THE MERRY WIDOWER** Hal Roach. Pathe. 2 Reels. James Finlayson. 1/8 (onlooker)

**BROMO AND JULIET** Hal Roach. Pathe. 2 Reels. Charley Chase. 19/9 (stagehand)

**THE CRUISE OF THE JASPER B** De Mille Pictures. Producers Distributing Corp. 6 Reels. Rod La Rocque, Mildred Harris. 31/12 (moving man)

## 1927

**ARE BRUNETTES SAFE?** Hal Roach. Pathe. 2 Reels. Charley Chase. 6/2 (villager)

**SEEING THE WORLD** Hal Roach. Pathe. 2 Reels. Our Gang. 13/2 (chauffeur in London sequence)

**FORGOTTEN SWEETIES** Hal Roach. Pathe. 2 Reels. Charley Chase 10/4 (porter)

**LOVE 'EM AND WEEP** Hal Roach. Pathe. 2 Reels. All Stars series. First of Charlie's 47 film appearances with Laurel & Hardy 12/6 (James Finlayson's butler)

**FLUTTERING HEARTS** Hal Roach. Pathe. 2 Reels. Charley Chase. 19/6 (roadside motorist under car)

**WITH LOVE AND HISSES** Hal Roach Pathe. 2 Reels L&H 27/8 (soldier at station)

**SUGAR DADDIES** Hal Roach. MGM. 2 Reels. All Stars. L&H 10/9 (hotel extra)

**COLLEGE** Joseph M.Schenck Productions. United Artists. 6 Reels. Buster Keaton. 10/9 (coxswain in race)

**THE SECOND HUNDRED YEARS** Hal Roach. MGM. 2 Reels. 8/10 All Stars – L&H. (convict)

**THE CALL OF THE CUCKOOS** Hal Roach. MGM. 2 Reels. Max Davidson series (with Laurel & Hardy, Charley Chase cameo appearances) 15/10 (asylum inmate)

**THE BATTLE OF THE CENTURY** Hal Roach. MGM. 2 Reels. L&H. 31/12 (Charlie has two parts in this film. As a spectator at the ringside and the pie delivery man)

## 1928

**PLAYIN' HOOKEY** Hal Roach. Pathe. 2 Reels. Our Gang l/1 (movie actor)

**LEAVE 'EM LAUGHING** Hal Roach. MGM. 2 Reels. L&H 28/1 (landlord)

**DRESSED TO KILL** Fox Film Corp. 7 Reels. Edmund Lowe, Mary Astor. 18/3 (uncredited)

**YOU'RE DARN TOOTIN'** Hal Roach. MGM. 2 Reels. L&H 21/4 (bandstand musician)

**LADY BE GOOD** First National Pictures. Jack Mullhall. (backstage actor in blackface)

**CROOKS CAN'T WIN** FBO. Pictures. 7 Reels. Ralph Lewis, Thelma Hill. 7/5 ('Bull' Savage, leader of marauders)

**SHOULD MARRIED MEN GO HOME** Hal Roach. MGM 2 Reels. L&H 8/9.(soda jerk)

**THE BUTTER AND EGG MAN** First National Pictures. Jack Mullhall 23/9 (pickpocket)

**CAPTAIN SWAGGER** Pathe Exchange. 7 Reels. Rod La Rocque, Sue Carol 14/10 (messenger fiddled out of tip by La Rocque & friend)

**TWO TARS** Hal Roach. MGM. 2 Reels. L&H 3/11 (shopkeeper who owns bubblegum machine)

**MUST WE MARRY?** (aka UK: ONE EMBARRASSING NIGHT) Trinity Pictures. 6 Reels. Pauline Garon, Lorraine Eason

**LOVE OVER NIGHT** Pathe Exchange. Rod La Rocque 25/11 (bellhop)

**FEED 'EM AND WEEP** Hal Roach. MGM. 2 Reels. Max Davidson 8/12 (cook)

# 1929

**A PAIR OF TIGHTS** Hal Roach. MGM. 2 Reels. Marion Byron, Anita Garvin 2/2 (motorist in altercation)

**WRONG AGAIN** Hal Roach. MGM. 2 Reels. L&H 23/2 (neighbour)

**LOUD SOUP** Hal Roach. MGM. 2 Reels. Charley Chase 16/3 (pedestrian?)

**THAT'S MY WIFE** Hal Roach. MGM. 2 Reels. L&H 23/3 (waiter)

**BIG BUSINESS** Hal Roach. MGM. 2 Reels. L&H 20/4 (neighbour)

**MOVIE NIGHT** Hal Roach. MGM. 2 Reels. Charley Chase. 11/5 (cinema audience member)

**DOUBLE WHOOPEE** Hal Roach. 2 Reels. L&H 18/5 (taxi driver)

**LITTLE MOTHER** Hal Roach. MGM. 2 Reels. Our Gang. 1/6 (taxi driver)

**BERTH MARKS** Hal Roach. MGM. 2 Reels. L&H 1/6 Charlie's first appearance in a sound film – Laurel & Hardy's second talkie. (Charlie doesn't speak) (husband on train)

N.B. All releases from here are sound, unless noted as silent

**LEAPING LOVE** Hal Roach. MGM. 2 Reels. Charley Chase 22/6 (ambulance man)

**MEN O' WAR** Hal Roach. MGM. 2 Reels. L&H 29/6 (boater on lake)

**DADS DAY** Hal Roach, Edgar Kennedy. 2 Reels. 6'7 (bather)

**BOXING GLOVES** Hal Roach. MGM. 2 Reels. Our Gang. 9/9. (diner owner)

**THEY GO BOOM** Hal Roach MGM. 2 Reels. L&H 21/9 (landlord)

**WHY BRING THAT UP?** Paramount. Famous Lasky Corp. 10 Reels. George Moran, Charles Mack. 4/10 (tough)

**BACON GRABBERS** Hal Roach. MGM. 2 Reels. Silent L&H 19/10. (truck driver)

**THE HOOSE-GOW** Hal Roach. MGM. 2 reels. L&H 16/11 (treetop lookout)

**SKIRT SHY** Hal Roach. MGM. 2 Reels. Harry Langdon. 30/11 (postman)

**ANGORA LOVE** Hal Roach. MGM. 2 Reels. Silent L&H 14/12 (neighbour who gets involved in water fight)

## 1930

**THE REAL McCOY** Hal Roach. MGM. 2 Reels. Charley Chase. 1/2. (mountain man)

**BLOTTO** Hal Roach. MGM. 3 Reels. L&H 8/2 (cab driver at end)

**LA VIDA NOCTURNA** Hal Roach. MGM. 3 Reels. Expanded Spanish language version of BLOTTO

**UNE NUIT EXTRAVAGANTE** Hal Roach. MGM. 3 Reels. Expanded French language version of BLOTTO

**THE FIGHTING PARSON** Hal Roach. MGM. 2 Reels. Harry Langdon. 22/2 (waiter)

**PICK 'EM YOUNG** E. B. Derr Productions. Robert Agnew 4/5

**BELOW ZERO** Hal Roach. MGM. 2 Reels. L&H 26/4 (street sweeper)

**TIEMBLA Y TITUBEA** Hal Roach. MGM. 3 Reels. Expanded Spanish language version of BELOW ZERO

**BEAR SHOOTERS** Hal Roach. MGM. 2 Reels. Our Gang. 17/5 (one of bootleggers)

**FIFTY MILLION HUSBANDS** Hal Roach. MGM. 2 Reels. Charley Chase 24/5 (neighbour)

**FAST WORK** Hal Roach, Charley Chase. 28/6 (waiter)

**LET'S GO NATIVE** Paramount. 9 Reels Jack Oakie Jennette MacDonald 16/8 (mover)

**PUPS IS PUPS** Hal Roach. MGM. 2 Reels. Our Gang. 30/8 (orchestra leader)

**DOLLAR DIZZY** Hal Roach. MGM. 3 Reels. Charley Chase. 4/10 (bellhop)

**EL PRINCIPE DEL DOLAR** Hal Roach. MGM. 5 Reels. Expanded Spanish language version of DOLLAR DIZZY

**LES CHERCHEUSES D'OR** Hal Roach. MGM. 5 Reels. Expanded French language version of DOLLAR DIZZY

**ONLY SAPS WORK** Paramount. 9 Reels. Leon Errol 6/12 (waiter)

**NOCHE DE DUENDES** Hal Roach. MGM. 5 Reels. L&H expanded Spanish language version of THE LAUREL – HARDY MURDER CASE and BERTH MARKS

**DER SPUK UM MITTERNACHT** Hal Roach. MGM. 5 Reels. L&H expanded German language version of THE LAUREL – HARDY MURDER CASE and BERTH MARKS

**FEU MON ONCLE** Hal Roach. MGM. 5 Reels. L&H expanded French language version of THE LAUREL – HARDY MURDER CASE and BERTH MARKS. (husband on train in **BERTH MARKS** footage in all versions)

## 1931

**BE BIG** Hal Roach. MGM. 3 Reels. L&H 7/2 (bellboy)

**LAS CALAVERAS** Hal Roach. MGM. 6 Reels. L&H Spanish language version of BE BIG and LAUGHING GRAVY

**LES CAROTTIERS** Hal Roach. MGM. 6 Reels. L&H French language version of BE BIG and LAUGHING GRAVY (bellboy in BE BIG; landlord in LAUGHING GRAVY footage in all versions)

**POLITIQUERIAS** Hal Roach. MGM. 6 Reels. L&H expanded Spanish language version of CHICKENS COME HOME (elevator boy – N.B. not in original US version)

**DELICIOUS** Fox Film Corp. 11 Reels. Janet Gaynor, Charles Farrell 26/2 (policeman)

**THE PIP FROM PITTSBURGH** Hal Roach. MGM. 2 Reels. Charley Chase. 21/3 (Kay's dancing partner)

**LIME JUICE NIGHTS** Larry Darmour Productions. 2 Reels. Karl Dane 22/3

**LAUGHING GRAVY** Hal Roach. MGM. 2 Reels. L&H 4/4. (landlord)

**ROUGH SEAS** Hal Roach. MGM. 3 Reels. Charley Chase (doughboy on deck)

**MONERIAS** Hal Roach. MGM. 4 Reels. Charley Chase. Expanded Spanish language version of ROUGH SEAS.

**AIR TIGHT** Hal Roach. 2 Reels. The Boyfriends series. 9/5 (glider owner)

**LETS DO THINGS** Hal Roach. MGM. 3 Reels. Thelma Todd, Zasu Pitts series. 6/6 (waiter)

**SWEEPSTAKES** RKO. 8 Reels. Eddie Quillan 10/7

**LEMON MERINGUE** RKO. Edgar Kennedy First of 'Average man' series. 3/8 (pieman)

**PARDON US** (aka JAILBIRDS) Hal Roach. MGM. 6 Reels. L&H 15/8 (dentist's assistant & delivery man)

**DE BOTE EN BOTE** Hal Roach. MGM. 7 Reels. An expanded Spanish language version of PARDON US

**SOUS LES VERROUS** Hal Roach. MGM. French language version of PARDON US

**HINTER SCHLOSS UND RIEGEL** Hal Roach. MGM. German language version of PARDON US

**MURAGLIE** Hal Roach. MGM. Italian language version of PARDON US

**THE PANIC IS ON** Hal Roach. MGM. 2 Reels. 15/8 Charley Chase. (pedestrian)

**SKIP THE MALOO** Hal Roach. MGM 9/9 (ship steward)

**COME CLEAN** Hal Roach. MGM. 2 Reels. L&H 19/9 (ice cream shop owner)

**BAD COMPANY** RKO. Pathe. 8 Reels. Helen Twelvetrees, Ricardo Cortez 2/10 (ships steward)

**THE PAJAMA PARTY** Hal Roach. MGM. 2 Reels. Todd, Pitts 3/10 (party guest)

**MAMA LOVES PAPA** Hal Roach. MGM. 2 Reels. The Boyfriends series 24/10 (milkman)

**SCRATCH AS CATCH CAN** RKO. 2 Reels. Clark and McCullough series 6/11

**WHAT A BOZO** Hal Roach. MGM. 2 Reels. Charley Chase. 7/11 (waiter)

**WAR MAMAS** Hal Roach. MGM. 2 Reels. Todd. Pitts 14/11 (bugle playing doughboy in one early shot-kisses hand through window)

**THE KICKOFF** Hal Roach. MGM. 2 Reels. The Boyfriends. 5/12 (man outside barber shop)

**BEAU HUNKS** (aka BEAU CHUMPS) Hal Roach. MGM. 4 Reels. L&H 12/12 (new recruit number 13)

**ON THE LOOSE** Hal Roach. MGM. 2 Reels. Todd, Pitts (with L&H cameo appearance) 26/12 (shooting gallery attendant)

## 1932

**SEAL SKINS** Hal Roach. MGM. 2 Reels. Todd, Pitts. 6/2 (one of 2 assumed seal thieves)

**LAW AND ORDER** (aka reissue title: GUNS A' BLAZING) Universal Pictures 7 Reels. John Huston, Harry Carey 7/2 (waiter in saloon)

**BON VOYAGE** RKO. 2 Reels. Edgar Kennedy 'Average Man' series 22/2 (steward)

**ANY OLD PORT** Hal Roach. MGM. 2 Reels. L&H 5/3 (boxing second)

**THE MUSIC BOX** Hal Roach. MGM. 3 Reels. L&H 16/4 (mail man)

**STRICTLY UNRELIABLE** Hal Roach. MGM. 2 Reels. Todd, Pitts 30/4 (stage manager)

**TOO MANY WOMEN** Hal Roach. MGM. 2 Reels. The Boyfriends. 14/5 (man in street hit by shoe)

**HOPPING OFF** Hal Roach. MGM. 2 Reels. Planned as the first of a possible new series teaming Charlie Hall with Charley Rogers as airplane pilots. Conflicting sources suggest the film was either abandoned after an accident when Rogers fell from a suspended plane, or was completed and previewed, but never released. Some footage was used in WILD BABIES, the last 'Boyfriends' short

**WILD BABIES** Hal Roach. MGM. 2 Reels. The Boyfriends 18/6 (explorer's man, Wellington)

**THE LOUD MOUTH** Mack Sennett. Paramount. 2 Reels. 17/6 (front row world series fan)

**WHAT PRICE HOLLYWOOD** RKO Pathe. 8 or 9 Reels. Constance Bennett, Lowell Sherman. 24/6 (reporter)

**MILLION DOLLAR LEGS** Paramount Publix Corp. 7 Reels. Jack Oakie, W.C.Fields, 8/7 (Klopstokian athlete)

**JUST A PAIN IN THE PARLOR** RKO. 2 Reels. Harry Sweet c3/8

**THE GOLF CHUMP** RKO. 2 Reels. Edgar Kennedy 5/8 (golfer)

**SHOW BUSINESS** Hal Roach MGM. 2 Reels. Todd, Pitts 20/8 (train passenger)

**YOUNG IRONSIDES** Hal Roach. MGM. 2 Reels. Charley Chase. 3/9 (bellboy)

**HOLD 'EM JAIL** RKO. Wheeler & Woolsey 16/9 (referee)

**PACK UP YOUR TROUBLES** Hal Roach. MGM. 6 Reels. L&H. 17/9 (janitor by dumb waiter)

**THE SOILERS** Hal Roach. MGM. 2 Reels. Todd, Pitts 29/10 (elevator boy)

**TAXI FOR TWO** Hal Roach. MGM. 2 Reels. Taxi Boys series. 3/12 (drunk)

**SNEAK EASILY** Hal Roach. MGM. 2 Reels. Todd, Pitts 10/12 (page)

**MR. BRIDE** Hal Roach. MGM. 2 Reels. Charley Chase 24/12 (tipsy ship's passenger)

**CYNARA** (aka reissue title: I WAS FAITHFUL) Howard Productions Inc. United Artists. 9 Reels. Ronald Colman, Kay Francis 24/12 (court spectator)

## 1933

**BRING 'EM BACK A WIFE** Hal Roach. MGM. 2 Reels. Taxi Boys.14/1 (taxi driver)

**FALLEN ARCHES** Hal Roach. MGM. 2 Reels. Charley Chase. 4/2 (hitchhiker)

**TWICE TWO** Hal Roach. MGM. 2 Reels. L&H 25/2 (delivery boy – delivers cake at end)

**MAIDS A LA MODE** Hal Roach. MGM. 2 Reels. Todd. Pitts 4/3 (party guest extra)

**RED NOSES** Hal Roach. MGM. 2 Reels. Todd Pitts. 19/3 (Charlie's part was cut)

**TAXI BARONS** Hal Roach. MGM. 2 Reels. Taxi Boys. 1/4 (butler at mansion)

**ME AND MY PAL** Hal Roach. MGM. 2 Reels. L&H. 22/4 (delivery boy – delivers wreath to wedding)

**HIS SILENT RACKET** Hal Roach. MGM. 2 Reels. Charley Chase. 29/4 (Brandenburg Cleaners man)

**KING KONG** RKO. 11 Reels. Fay Wray, Robert Armstrong. 7/5 (ships crew member)

**DIPLOMANIACS** RKO. 7 Reels. Wheeler and Woolsey 12/5. (Shaffner the valet)

**ONE TRACK MINDS** Hal Roach. MGM. 2 Reels. Todd, Pitts. 20/5 (train passenger extra)

**THE DRUGGIST'S DILEMMA** RKO. 2 Reels. Clark and McCullough. 23/5 (trapeze artist Charlie Zeno)

**THUNDERING TAXIS** Hal Roach. MGM. 2 Reels. Taxi Boys (taxi driver, B&B Taxis)

**THE MIDNIGHT PATROL** Hal Roach. MGM. 2 Reels. L&H 3/8 (accomplice of tyre thief)

**KICKIN THE CROWN AROUND** RKO. Bobby Clark. 2 Reels. 4/8 (Disputin's messenger)

**MORNING GLORY** RKO. 8 Reels. Katherine Hepburn 18/8 (actor)

**FLIRTING IN THE PARK** RKO. 2 Reels. Blondes and Redheads June Brewster 18/8 (boatman)

**THE MASQUERADER** (1933) Sam Goldwyn Inc. United Artists. 8 Reels. Ronald Colman, Elissa Landi. 2/9 (Charlie's part in this film was cut)

**BEAUTY AND THE BUS** Hal Roach. MGM. 2 Reels. Thelma Todd, Patsy Kelly series 16/9 (cinema usher on stage)

**RHAPSODY IN BREW** Hal Roach. MGM. 2 Reels. Musical. (advertised in at least one trade journal as an MGM Colortone Revue, so possibly made, though not generally released, in colour) 30/9 (waiter)

**BUSY BODIES** Hal Roach. MGM. 2 Reels. L&H 7/10 (sawmill worker)

**WHAT FUR** RKO. 2 Reels. Edgar Kennedy 'Average Man' series 3/11

**KEG O' MY HEART** Hal Roach. 2 Reels. 11/11 (waiter)

**BACKS TO NATURE** Hal Roach. MGM. 2 Reels. Todd, Kelly. 14/11 (hunter)

**LUNCHEON AT TWELVE** Hal Roach. MGM. 2 Reels. Charley Chase 9/12 (street sweeper)

**HOLD YOUR TEMPER** Columbia. 2 Reels. Leon Errol series 15/12

**SONS OF THE DESERT** (aka UK: FRATERNALLY YOURS) Hal Roach. MGM. 7 Reels. L&H. 29/12 (second waiter)

## 1934

**THE NEW DEALERS** Paramount. 2 Reels. Eugene Pallette 5/4

**THE UNDIE WORLD** RKO. 2 Reels. Blondes and Redheads 15/6 (nightclub waiter)

**DERBY DECADE** RKO. Ruth Etting 12/7 (barfly)

**OLIVER THE EIGHTH** Hal Roach. MGM. 3 Reels. L&H 13/1 (Charlie's part as laundryman cut)

**BRIDAL BAIL** RKO. 2 Reels. 'Blondes and Redheads' series 9/2 (irate movie patron)

**BABES IN THE GOODS** Hal Roach. MGM. 2 Reels. Todd, Kelly 10/2 (spectator in crowd at shop window)

**LOVE ON A LADDER** RKO. 2 Reels. Edgar Kennedy Average Man series. 2/3 (man in pool room)

**HI' NEIGHBOR** Hal Roach. MGM. 2 Reels. Our Gang 3/3 (window washer)

**SOUP AND FISH** Hal Roach. MGM. 2 Reels. Todd, Kelly 31/3 (second butler, announcing guests)

**APPLES TO YOU** Hal Roach, Billy Gilbert 7/4 (stagehand)

**I'LL TAKE VANILLA** Hal Roach. MGM. 2 Reels. Charley Chase 5/5 (cop)

**MAID IN HOLLYWOOD** Hal Roach. MGM. 2 Reels. Todd, Kelly 19/5 (cameraman)

**MOVIE DAZE** Hal Roach. MGM. 2 Reels. All Star series – first of the talkie All Star series to go into production 26/5 (assistant director in studio)

**CALL IT LUCK** Fox Film Corp. 7 Reels. 'Pat' Peterson, Herbert Mundin. 1/6 (detective)

**MUSIC IN YOUR HAIR** Hal Roach. MGM. 2 Reels. Musical. 2/6 (cab driver)

**COCKEYED CAVALIERS** RKO. 8 Reels. Wheeler and Woolsey. 29/6 (coach driver)

**IT HAPPENED ONE DAY** Hal Roach. MGM. 2 Reels. Charley Chase 7/7 (office clerk)

**THEM THAR HILLS** Hal Roach. MGM. 2 Reels. L&H. 21/7 (Mr. Hall who needs gas)

**MIKE FRIGHT** Hal Roach. MGM. 2 Reels. Our Gang 25/7 (elevator boy)

**ONE HORSE FARMERS** Hal Roach. MGM. 2 Reels. Todd, Kelly 1/9 (subway passenger)

**SOMETHING SIMPLE** Hal Roach. MGM. 2 Reels. Charley Chase 8/9 (one of two sanitarium men)

**OPENED BY MISTAKE** Hal Roach. MGM. 2 Reels. Todd, Kelly. 6/10 (hospital intern)

**THE GAY DIVORCEE** RKO. Pandro S. Berman Production. RKO. 7 Reels. Fred Astaire, Ginger Rogers 19/10 (messenger at dock)

**FITS IN A FIDDLE** RKO. 2 Reels. Clark & McCullough. 20/10 (musician in orchestra)

**KENTUCKY KERNELS** (aka UK: DOUBLE TROUBLE) RKO. 9 Reels. Wheeler and Woolsey. 2/11 (cigarette stand owner)

**KID MILLIONS** Howard Productions. United Artists. 10 reels. Eddie Cantor, Ann Sothern. 10/11 (native)

**BABES IN TOYLAND** (aka: reissue MARCH OF THE WOODEN SOLDIERS) Hal Roach. MGM. 8 Reels. L&H 30/11 (one of townspeople)

**THE LIVE GHOST** Hal Roach. MGM. 2 Reels. L&H 8/12 (sailor in saloon)

**THE CHASES OF PIMPLE STREET** 22 December, Hal Roach. MGM. 2 Reels. Charley Chase 22/12 (man in street)

## 1935

**TIT FOR TAT** Hal Roach. MGM. 2 Reels. L&H. 5/1 (Mr. Hall, grocer)

**TREASURE BLUES** Hal Roach. MGM. 2 Reels. Todd, Kelly. 26/1 (delivery man)

**OKAY TOOTS** Hal Roach. MGM. 2 Reels. Charley Chase. 2/2 (irate man)

**BEGINNERS LUCK** Hal Roach. MGM. 2 Reels. Our Gang 23/2 (stage hand)

**SING, SISTER, SING** Hal Roach. MGM. 2 Reels. Todd, Kelly 2/3 (baggage clerk)

**POKER AT EIGHT** Hal Roach. MGM. 2 Reels. Charley Chase. 9/3 (waiter)

**THICKER THAN WATER** Hal Roach. MGM. 2 Reels. L&H 16/3 (bank teller)

**SOUTHERN EXPOSURE** Hal Roach. MGM. 2 Reels. Charley Chase. 6/4 (yokel extra sitting in background & in court)

**TEACHERS BEAU** Hal Roach. MGM. 2 Reels. Our Gang. 27/5 (party guest)

**BONNIE SCOTLAND** Hal Roach. MGM. 8 Reels. L&H. 23/8 (native henchman)

**IN LOVE AT 40** RKO. 2 Reels. Edgar Kennedy 'Average Man' series 30/8 (barbershop customer with one line)

**TOP HAT** RKO. 11 Reels. Fred Astaire, Ginger Rogers. 6/9 (extra)

**TWIN TRIPLETS** Hal Roach. MGM. 2 Reels. Todd, Kelly 12/10 (ambulance attendant)

**ANNIE OAKLEY** RKO. 10 Reels Barbara Stanwyck, Preston Foster 15/11 (drunk in saloon)

**HOT MONEY** Hal Roach. MGM. 2 Reels. Todd, Kelly 16/11 (tenant)

## 1936

**THE PINCH SINGER** Hal Roach. MGM. 2 Reels. Our Gang 4/1 (druggist & audience extra)

**ALL AMERICAN TOOTHACHE** Hal Roach. MGM. 2 Reels. Todd, Kelly 25/1 (dental college inmate)

**THE BOHEMIAN GIRL** Hal Roach. MGM. 7 Reels. L&H. 4/2. (voiceover only by Charlie for gypsy offering congratulations)

**NEIGHBORHOOD HOUSE** Hal Roach. MGM. 2 Reels. (produced and previewed as a 6 Reel feature, but released only as a 2 Reel short). Charley Chase. 9/5 (usher on stage)

**SWING TIME** RKO. 12 Reels. Fred Astaire, Ginger Rogers. 4/9 (taxi driver)

**OUR RELATIONS** Hal Roach. MGM. 8 reels. L&H 30/10 (pawnshop extra) N.B. Foxy Hall also extra in nightclub or beer garden scenes

**KELLY THE SECOND** Hal Roach Patsy Kelly (Charlie's part as a ring attendant may have been cut from this film)

## 1937

**SHALL WE DANCE** RKO. 12 Reels. Fred Astaire, Ginger Rogers. 7/5 (ship's bartender)

**PICK A STAR** Hal Roach. MGM. 7 Reels. Rosina Lawrence, Jack Haley, L&H. 21/5 (assistant director in studio)

**THE BIG SQUIRT** Columbia Pictures. 2 Reels. Charley Chase 17/9 (man in crowd)

## 1938

**HEY! HEY! USA** Gainsborough Pictures General Film. 9 Reels. Will Hay (Leary's pal, Lefty)

## 1939

**FIVE CAME BACK** RKO. 7 Reels. Chester Morris, Lucille Ball. 23/6 (airport worker)

**MAN ABOUT TOWN** Paramount Pictures. 9 Reels. Jack Benny, Dorothy Lamour 7/7 (stage pageboy/ Bob's assistant)

**BACHELOR MOTHER** RKO. 8 Reels. Ginger Rogers, David Niven. 4/8 (dance hall customer)

**THE HUNCHBACK OF NOTRE DAME** RKO. 11 Reels. Charles Laughton, Maureen O'Hara 29/12 (mercury) (Charlie's part was cut from this film)

## 1940

**MEXICAN SPITFIRE** RKO. 7 Reels. Lupe Velez, Leon Errol. 12/1. First of Mexican Spitfire series (elevator boy)

**VIGIL IN THE NIGHT** RKO. 10 Reels. Carole Lombard, Brian Aherne 9/2 (extra at hearing)

**SLIGHTLY AT SEA** RKO. 2 Reels. Edgar Kennedy 'Average Man' series. 9/2 (garage owner – sells Ed his own tyre)

**A CHUMP AT OXFORD** Hal Roach. United Artists. 4 Reels (USA), 6 Reels (Europe). L&H. 16/2 (Oxford student, Hector)

**CURTAIN CALL** RKO. 6 Reels. Barbara Read, Alan Mowbray. (second waiter)

**PRIMROSE PATH** RKO. Ginger Rodgers 22/4 (man in diner)

**SAPS AT SEA** Hal Roach. United Artists. 6 Reels. L&H. 3/5. (desk clerk) Charlie's last appearance with L&H

**YOU CAN'T FOOL YOUR WIFE** RKO. 8 Reels. 21/5 (Ritz Amsterdam bellhop)

**MILLIONAIRES IN PRISON** RKO. 7 Reels. Lee Tracy, Linda Hayes 12/7 (cockney convict heckler)

**TRAILER TRAGEDY** RKO. 2 Reels. Edgar Kennedy 'Average Man' series. 18/10 (camper who meets Ed in washroom)

**ONE NIGHT IN THE TROPICS** Universal. 9 Reels. Abbott & Costello. 15/11 (second S.S.Atlantica steward)

**MEXICAN SPITFIRE OUT WEST** RKO. 8 Reels. Lupe Velez, Leon Errol. 29/11. (elevator boy)

**DRAFTED IN THE DEPOT** RKO. 2 Reels. Edgar Kennedy 'Average Man' series 20/12 (man who uniform to Ed)

## 1941

**THEY MET IN ARGENTINA** RKO. Maureen O'Hara 25/4 (sailor in cantina brawl)

**A POLO PHONY** RKO. 2 Reels. Leon Errol series. 16/5

**AN APPLE IN HIS EYE** RKO. 2 Reels. Edgar Kennedy 'Average Man' series. 6/6 (Edgar's neighbour)

**SAN ANTONIO ROSE** Universal Jane Frazee 20/6 (waiter)

**MAN I CURED** RKO. 2 Reels. Leon Errol series 26/9 (taxi driver)

**I'LL FIX IT** RKO. 2 Reels. Edgar Kennedy 'Average Man' series 7/10 (laundryman)

**TOP SERGEANT MULLIGAN** Monogram Pictures Corp. 7 Reels. Nat Pendleton, Carol Hughes. 17/10 (Bud Doolittle)

**NIAGARA FALLS** Hal Roach. United Artists. 5 Reels. Zasu Pitts, Slim Summerville. 17/10 (bellhop)

**CADET GIRL** 20th Century Fox. Carole Landis 28/11 (soldier at camp show)

**A QUIET FOURTH** RKO. ?? Reels. Edgar Kennedy 'Average Man' series. 19/12 (Ed's neighbour)

**FATHER STEPS OUT** Monogram Pictures Corp. 7 Reels. (remake of the 1934 CITY LIMITS) Frank Albertson, Jed Prouty. 19/12 (hobo 'Nap', aka Napoleon)

## 1942

**THE MAN FROM HEADQUARTERS** Monogram Pictures Corp. 7 Reels. Frank Albertson, Joan Woodbury. 23/1 (news photographer)

**SING YOUR WORRIES AWAY** RKO. Bert Lahr 6/3 (waiter)

**HITTING THE HEADLINES** Republic Pictures. Abert Dekker 13/3 (gaffer)

**FRAMING FATHER** RKO. 2 Reels. Leon Errol series. 15/5 (waiter in Silver Slipper club)

**THE FALCON TAKES OVER** RKO. George Sanders (Louie – waiter in
  Swan Club)
**TWO FOR THE MONEY** RKO. 2 Reels. Edgar Kennedy 'Average Man'
  series 14/8
**POLICE BULLETS** Monogram Pictures. Joan Marsh 25/9 (rabbit, Duke's
  short thug)
**CRIMINAL INVESTIGATOR** Monogram Pictures Robert Lowery 22/10
  (soapy)
**ROUGH ON RENTS** RKO. 2 Reels. Edgar Kennedy 'Average Man' series.
  30/10 (Mr. Jones who Ed owes $80)
**SEVEN DAYS LEAVE** RKO. Victor Mature 13/11 (waiter)

## 1943

**THE APE MAN (aka LOCK YOUR DOORS)** Monogram Pictures Corp.
  Bela Lugosi 5/3 (Barney the photographer)
**GEM JAMS** RKO. 2 Reels. Leon Errol series. 19/3 (waiter)
**HONEYMOON LODGE** Universal. David Bruce 23/7 (hotel handyman)
**SHOT IN THE ESCAPE** Columbia. 2 Reels. Billy Gilbert, Cliff Nazarro.
  6/8 (Harry)
**SO'S YOUR UNCLE** Universal. Billie Burke 1/9 (waiter)
**WHO'S HUGH** Columbia. 2 Reels. Hugh Herbert. 17/12 (waiter)

## 1944

**THE LODGER** 20th Century Fox. 9 Reels. Laird Cregar, George Sanders.
  7/1 (singer on stage)
**WEEKEND PASS** Universal. Martha O'Driscoll 14/2 (man hit by tomato)
**LOVE YOUR LANDLORD** RKO. 2 Reels. Edgar Kennedy 'Average Man'
  series. 3/3 (head of family who move into Ed's apartment while they're
  trying to move out)
**RADIO RAMPAGE** RKO. 2 Reels. Edgar Kennedy 'Average Man' series.
  28/3 (radio repair man whose bill Ed won't pay)
**GIRLS, GIRLS, GIRLS** RKO. 2 Reels. Leon Errol series. 9/6 (waiter
  knocked down twice in hall)
**THE CANTERVILLE GHOST** MGM. Charles Laughton (Bold Sir Guy's
  squire)
**HI BEAUTIFUL** Universal. Martha O'Driscoll 18/12 (milkman)

# 1945

**SHE GETS HER MAN** Universal. Joan Davis 12/1 (man in painter gag)
**HANGOVER SQUARE** 20th Century Fox. 8 Reels. Laird Cregar, Linda
  Darnell. 7/2 (singer in pub)
**HER LUCKY NIGHT** Universal. Patty Andrews 9/2 (window washer)
**ON STAGE EVERYBODY** Universal. Jack Oakie 13/7 (painter)
**RADIO STARS ON DEMAND** RKO. Wally Brown 1/8 (apparently
  Charlie's part as the front end of a horse, has been deleted)
**MAMA LOVES PAPA** RKO. 6 Reels. Leon Errol, Elisabeth Risdon. 8/8
  (bartender)
**THE CRIMSON CANARY** Universal. Noah Beery 9/11 (undetermined role)
**CONFIDENTIAL AGENT** Warner Bros. Lauren Bacall 10/11

# 1946

**WITHOUT RESERVATIONS** (aka: THANKS GOD, I'LL TAKE IT
  FROM HERE) RKO. 12 Reels. Claudette Colbert, John Wayne. 3/6
  (window cleaner in newsreel at start)
**DRESSED TO KILL** (aka UK: SHERLOCK HOLMES AND THE
  SECRET CODE) Universal Pictures. 8 Reels. Basil Rathbone, Nigel
  Bruce. 7/6 (cab driver)
**WALL STREET BLUES** RKO. 2 Reels. Edgar Kennedy 'Average Man'
  series 12/7 (house painter )
**SISTER KENNY** RKO. Rosalind Russell 10/10 (airport attendant)
**ABIE'S IRISH ROSE** Bing Crosby Productions. 27/12 (hotel porter)

# 1948

**HOW TO CLEAN HOUSE** RKO. 2 Reels. Edgar Kennedy 'Average Man'
  series 14/5 (milkman)
**HOME CANNING** RKO. 2 Reels. Edgar Kennedy 'Average Man' series.
  16/8 (painter)

# 1950

**THE VISCIOUS YEARS** Emerald Productions. Film Classics Inc. 8 Reels.
  Tommy Cook, Sybil Merritt 10/3

**THE MILKMAN** Universal International. 9 Reels. Donald O'Connor, Jimmy Durante. 17/10 (Ed)

**SPOOKY WOOKY** RKO. 2 Reels. Leon Errol series. 1/12 (one of 2 strangers sizing up house)

# 1952

**ANDROCLES AND THE LION** RKO. Jean Simmons 9/1 (town crier)

**LIMELIGHT** Celebrated Films, United Artists. 13 Reels. Charlie Chaplin, Claire Bloom 23/10. (newspaper seller on street)

# 1953

**ROGUE'S MARCH MGM** Peter Lawford 13/2 (batman)

# 1955

**ILLEGAL** Warner Bros. 9 Reels. Edward G.Robinson, Nina Foch 20/8 (bellhop)

# 1956

**SO YOU WANT TO PLAY THE PIANO** Warner Bros. 1 Reel. 'Joe McDoakes series' with George O'Hanlon. 5/5 (Clyde – piano removal man)

Extracts with Charlie Hall also appear in the following compilation films:

**THE GOLDEN AGE OF COMEDY** 1958
**WHEN COMEDY WAS KING** 1960
**LAUREL & HARDY'S LAUGHING TWENTIES** 1965
**THE CRAZY WORLD OF LAUREL & HARDY** 1966
**THE FURTHER PERILS OF LAUREL & HARDY** 1967
**THE BEST OF LAUREL & HARDY**
**FOUR CLOWNS** 1970

Charlie may also have appeared in the following films:

**MADAME MYSTERY** (1926) Hal Roach.
**THE BARGAIN OF THE CENTURY** (1933) Hal Roach. MGM. 2 Reels. Todd, Pitts 9/4

**CITY LIMITS** (1934) Monogram Pictures Corp. William T.Lackey
Production. Monogram. 7 Reels. Frank Craven, Sally Blane. 1/5
**HOLLYWOOD HOTEL** (1938) Warner Bros. Pictures; First National.
Warner Bros. 12 Reels. Dick Powell, Rosemary Lane. 15/1
**BOYFRIEND** (1939) 20th Century Fox. Film Corp. 7 Reels. Jane Withers,
Arleen Whelan. 19/5
**HOLD YOUR TEMPER** (1943) RKO. 2 Reels. Edgar Kennedy 'Average
Man' series. 15/12
**CRAZY LIKE A FOX** (1944) Columbia. 2 Reels. Billy Gilbert. 1/5
**FOREVER AMBER** (1947) 20th Century Fox. 14 Reels. Linda Darnell
22/10

# CHARLIE HALL FAMILY TREE

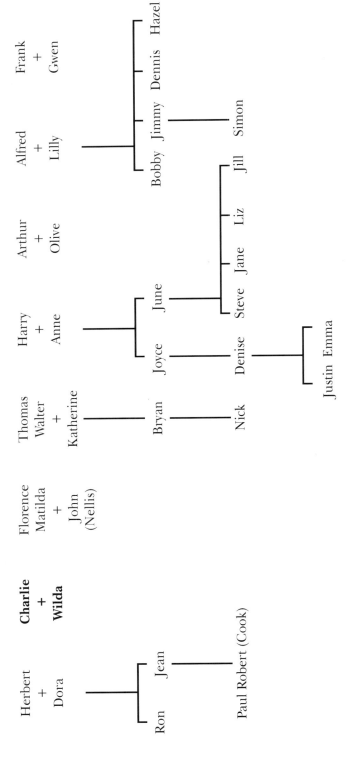